Simple Fare

Simple Fare

Karen Mordechai of Sunday Suppers

A guide to everyday cooking and eating

Abrams, New York

Spring Summer

Writing + Photography: Karen Mordechai
Styling: Karen Mordechai

Concept + Graphic Design: Marjolein Delhaas (marjoleindelhaas.com)
Styling + Editorial Assistants: Lara Southern + Julia Johnson

Editor: Laura Dozier
Production Manager: True Sims

Library of Congress Control Number: 2016943556

ISBN: 978-1-4197-2414-5

Printed and bound in China
10 9 8 7 6 5 4 3 2 1

Abrams books are available at special discounts when purchased
in quantity for premiums and promotions as well as fundraising or
educational use. Special editions can also be created to specification.
For details, contact specialsales@abramsbooks.com or the address below.

ABRAMS The Art of Books
115 West 18th Street, New York, NY 10011
abramsbooks.com

Essentials
20

Bread
half-day rye
22

Guide to Cooking Grains
25

Eggs, a guide
26

Garlic Confit
thyme, lemon peel
28

Basic Vegetable Stock
30

Pickles
31

Pickled Red Onion
32

Pickled Mustard Seeds
32

Breakfast
34

Poached Eggs
black quinoa, toasted buckwheat, kefir, fermented kraut, pepita
36

Fruit Salad
cantaloupe, rainier cherry, golden raspberry, ricotta
38

Green Shakshuka
wild greens, leek, za'atar oil, yogurt
41

Breakfast Board
salmon, trout, whitefish roe, crème fraîche, sumac red onion
44

Buttered Eggs
rye, pecorino, lemon
46

Soft-Boiled Eggs
labneh, breakfast radish, pine nut
48

Slow-Cooked Oat Porridge
honeycomb, white sesame, chamomile, cyprus salt
50

Smoothie Bowl
espresso, maca, cinnamon, maple, banana, almond milk
52

Toast and Roasted Fruit Jam
blueberry, balsamic, basil
54

Wilted Flower Yogurt Bowl
petals, pistachio, black sesame, maple
56

Buckwheat Bread
whipped ricotta, rose honey
58

Ricotta Pancakes
blackberry, thyme, crème fraîche, hazelnut
60

Toasts
62

Avocado Toast
watermelon radish, mustard seed, pickled red onion, pink salt
64

Mushroom Toast
beech, thyme, sancerre
66

Ramp Toast
ramp butter, roasted ramp
68

Pan con Tomate
roma tomato, olive oil-fried miche
70

Eggplant Crostini
black garlic, tahini, pine nut, pickled red onion
72

Poached Salmon Toast
herb pesto, lemon, pink salt
75

Bowls
78

Parmesan Brodo
egg, young spinach, radish
80

Everyday Bowl
farro, market radish, roasted purple carrot, watercress dressing, piave
82

White Miso Soup
soba noodle, black trumpet mushroom, bok choy, beet-cured egg
84

Plates
86

Ceviche
halibut, yellowfin tuna, red onion, kaffir lime, poblano, crispy garlic
88

Spring Salad
zucchini crudo, buffalo mozzarella, lemon balm, almond
90

Grilled Octopus
burnt citrus crema, braised olive, parsley
92

Smoked Black Bread Panzanella
beet, purple kale, radicchio, smoked ricotta, saba
94

Deconstructed Niçoise Salad
market lettuce, halibut, potato, haricot vert, braised olive, soft egg
97

contents

This is how I cook.

This is how we eat.

Concept

This book is meant to be a resource, a guide for cooking seasonally and simply.

I am drawn to food and its inherent beauty. In this book, I have collected a sampling of the way I like to cook, daily—both at our studio and for my family. The recipes are seasonally inspired, good, and wholesome. It is food as it should be: nuanced, bright, and gorgeous. This is about how we cook and eat every day in our home and with our loved ones.

Journey

I grew up surrounded by food, as it was the backbone of immigrant traditions in a new environment. My family brought their cultures and traditions and expressed their love through meals of plenty. Their story (and their food) was a complex and varied one rooted in Jerusalem in the 1950s, a time in which ethnicities from around the globe were melding together in a young country. Influences from the Middle East and Eastern Europe were converging to formulate a new community. When my family then immigrated to the United States, they brought these melded cultures with them. As I developed my own viewpoint, these influences, along with my current journey, created my own path. I was always fascinated with food. I was drawn to its beauty and also moved by its cultural significance. I studied as a photographer, and in 2005 I did my master's thesis on the food in my home, through the scope of its maternal lineage.

A few years later, I began Sunday Suppers, a communal cooking space, and became more and more immersed in the world of food. I was photographing and also cooking. Exploring, eating, and finding my own sense of things. I met amazing chefs and cooks, and was continually inspired in our collaborative atmosphere.

Sunday Suppers evolved into a hub and a center point for community and inspiration. At the space, we hold community dinners and events that bring people into the kitchen. The premise is to cook together and enjoy the culture and beauty of food through connectivity.

I believe food should capture your spirit. Your food, I believe, is a compilation of your journey in life— it collects bits and pieces as you go.

From youth and culture, from travel, and from day-to-day experiences. It is also, very much, an evolution. My own story and viewpoint sit on the pages ahead.

As you read, I hope you will see a true love and celebration of food. That is what this book is about. My hope is that it liberates you and allows you to learn a few great techniques that will honestly make you a better cook. More than anything, I hope it inspires you to find the same joy in cooking as I do.

Food's ability to bring people together is unparalleled. It is at the foundation of our cultures; it is the goodness we can bring to ourselves and others. When we celebrate food and retain its inherent quality, we nourish ourselves and our lives. We take the time to source good ingredients and produce. We support our local farmers and artisans, and we help sustain a beautiful cycle of goodness that extends to the people around us.

Food

At Sunday Suppers, I've had the opportunity to experience and make food as a cultural connector. At the studio, we create food that is gorgeous and fun and sometimes off-beat. We cook all the time, and we experiment with colors and flavors. Sometimes these are simple studio meals, and other times they are larger community dinners for twenty to fifty people. Food, in our studio, brings people together: It is a day-to-day community affair.

As a mother, I cook almost all our meals (yes, even after long studio days). I feel this is important, and it is how I can nourish my (little) family and myself. I know where my food is coming from: I try to buy seasonally, from farmers and local purveyors. With all this said, I also know the challenges of a very busy schedule and weekday life. And so I have found my way: making grains and a soup on a Sunday night, and sometimes roasting some vegetables for the week. I'll often make double the amount of dressing so we can have it in the refrigerator. I keep lots of greens, eggs, avocados, and fresh breads on hand at home.

Format

Ultimately, the purpose of this book is to compile all these meals from the studio and our home and bring them forth as a resource for simple and beautiful food. The journey is unending, but this is a starting point. This book will be a two-volume one, with *Fall / Winter* upcoming.

Each family and home has their own story, their own way. If there is a contribution to be made here, it is simply to tell our path and food story. If it happens to inspire you to cook, to visit a market, and to experiment beyond the norm, that would be an achievement.

The recipes are meant to be utilitarian and straightforward, but simultaneously unique and inspiring. The word *simple* is used often and is meant to impart a sense of ease, not intended to be simplistic—these recipes are aimed to be inspiring without being out of reach. Aspirational and liberating.

Cook with your season, and in your way. Have freedom and lightness in your kitchen; it's a wonderful place to be.

Usage/
Market
Variations

I hear from many cooks that they will follow a recipe to a T; they will create their list and take on a recipe like it is a didactic thing.

Here, we are breaking the mold a bit. If you go to market with the intention to make an oyster mushroom risotto, but the mushrooms are not looking great, or there are no oyster mushrooms in season, you can make an alternate decision.

Instead of mushrooms, sage, and Pecorino for your risotto, choose fennel, Parmesan, and thyme. The idea here is to offer alternates, which we call "market variations," based on the season and also to give readers guidance on some flavor profiles that work. In this way, readers can feel liberated.

Each recipe is built with a few seasonal items, herbs, and flavorings. These original ingredients are underlined. Beneath the recipe title, you will find two or three alternate versions of the original ingredients. These variations can be substituted for the underlined ingredients and are listed in the same order as the items that they are replacing in the recipe title. Unless otherwise noted, the alternate ingredients can be prepared and incorporated into the finished dish in the same manner as the original.

To help you utilize the market variations in the book, there is a "Cook's Notes" section (see page 171) that offers measurements and additional information on how to prepare the variations. Be sure to reference that section for further assistance when making a recipe with a variant ingredient.

Seasonality

Cooking seasonally means supporting our local farmers and producers. It also means celebrating produce at its peak and best form.

There is a natural rhythm to the markets and the seasons. In winter, we stay closer to the home and cook warm and nurturing meals. Most of the produce is in the form of root vegetation, some greens, and limited fruits. As the weather warms, new and exciting produce starts to become available. Ramps, morels, and rhubarb make their appearance, as well as peas, alliums, and other vibrant greens. In summer we find berries and tomatoes and stone fruit. The market quite literally blooms. Of course, there are no hard-and-fast rules; some cities and climates offer varied seasonal produce, but this is the general format, give or take.

These recipes will guide you through the *Spring/Summer* offerings at your local markets, as they tend to unfold in different locales. As there is always a transition between seasons, you'll find that reflected in the meals. Slowly, as the weather warms, we begin to lighten our meals a bit, but the beginning of spring can still be chilly. We ease into the season. Some of the dishes are warm and soothing, while others are lighter, cooler options. As your personal surroundings change, your cooking often reflects those changes.

Essentials

In this section, you will find the building blocks of our kitchen. These are the foundations of our meals, and great things to stock your larder with. At the beginning of the week, usually on a Sunday evening, I will make a stock, a grain, or pickles to keep in the refrigerator for the week. The beauty is having them at the ready on busy weekdays to enlighten or enhance your meals, but also to speed things up a bit. You will also find practical guidance: a guide to grain cooking and one on making eggs properly. These things are so useful to have in your culinary repertoire and will allow you to cook intuitively. Removing the guesswork lets you have more fun with the recipes in the following chapters.

Bread, half-day rye

Bread

half-day rye

Makes 1 loaf

We love an artisanal bread from a local bakery, but on a day when you have the urge to bake, this bread is a wonder—crusty on the outside and pillow-like in the interior. While a classic bread recipe can take several days to prepare, this one requires merely a half day to make and rise, and will become a go-to for everyday usage. Use high-quality milled rye flour for best results. Serve toasted and well buttered.

3¼ cups plus 2 tablespoons (340 g) rye flour
3 cups (375 g) all-purpose flour, plus more for dusting
1 tablespoon active dry yeast
3½ teaspoons (17 g) kosher salt
4 teaspoons sugar
1 tablespoon unsalted butter

In a large bowl, whisk together the flours, yeast, salt, and sugar until well combined. Add 3 cups (720 ml) room-temperature water and mix with a wooden spoon until a shaggy, sticky dough forms. Cover bowl with plastic wrap and set in a warm, draft-free place to rest for 4 hours.

Butter a 16 x 4-inch (approximately 40.5 x 10-cm) extra-long loaf pan. Turn the dough out onto a well-floured work surface. With floured hands, and handling the dough as little as possible, gently shape into an approximate 16 x 12-inch (40.5 x 30-cm) rectangle. Fold the rectangle into thirds, as you would a letter, to form a long, narrow loaf, about the size of the loaf pan. Carefully lower the dough into the loaf pan and cover loosely with a clean dish towel; place in a warm, draft-free place to rise for an hour, or until the loaf has doubled in size.

Preheat the oven to 425°F (220°C). Remove the dish towel from the pan and, using a fine-mesh sieve, lightly dust the top of the loaf with flour. Transfer it to the oven and bake until golden brown, about 25 minutes.

Transfer the bread to a wire rack and let cool in the loaf pan for 5 minutes. Invert the pan to remove the bread and allow to cool completely.

Storage – *Best enjoyed immediately. If storage is necessary, keep in a sealed bag.*

Guide to Cooking Grains

Healthful grains are a great thing to have on hand. I tend to make a pot weekly and keep it handy to add to an everyday bowl, salad, or even soup. It makes the meals hearty and enriching. Choosing well-milled quality grains is important for both nutrition and taste. You may use water or any stock of your preference to infuse additional flavor.

In a medium saucepan, heat 1 tablespoon olive oil over medium-low heat. Add the grain of your choice and toast in the saucepan until lightly golden and fragrant, 2 to 3 minutes. Add the water (or stock) and a pinch of salt and bring to a boil. Reduce the heat to low, cover, and cook for the time indicated by the chart. Remove from the heat, leave grains covered for 5 minutes, and fluff the grains before serving or using in a recipe. If you are making farro, simply drain any excess water before serving. If you are cooking more than 1 cup of a grain, use a ratio of 1 cup grain to 1 tablespoon olive oil to toast it.

Grain to water (or stock) ratio:

quinoa*
1 : 1¾ cups (170 g : 420 ml)
25 minutes

farro
1 : 3 cups (200 g : 720 ml)
30 minutes

bulgur
1 : 2 cups (140 g : 480 ml)
15 minutes

short-grain brown rice
1 : 2 cups (190 g : 480 ml)
45 minutes

long-grain white rice
1 : 1½ cups (180 g : 360 ml)
20 minutes

* Make sure to rinse quinoa very well before cooking to remove the naturally occurring but unpleasant-tasting chemical saponin that coats the grains.

Eggs, a guide

A beautifully prepared egg is a staple in many of our bowls, toasts, and other dishes, enriching a meal with protein and creaminess. When poaching, the goal is to achieve the perfect oval: white on the outside, oozy on the inside. For frying or boiling, getting the yolk to the preferred doneness determines its perfection. These are our methods, tried and true for both single and multiple preparations.

fried, Makes 1 egg

1 tablespoon unsalted butter or olive oil
1 egg

In a small nonstick sauté pan, melt the butter over medium-low heat. Swirl the pan so its surface is completely coated. Crack the egg into a ramekin and gently slide it from the ramekin into the middle of the pan. Cook until the white is opaque and set, 2 to 3 minutes. Using a spatula, gently flip the egg and cook on the second side to the desired doneness, about 30 seconds longer for a runny yolk, 1 to 2 minutes for a partly set yolk, and 3 to 5 minutes for a fully cooked yolk. Test for doneness by very gently pressing the yolk once the egg is flipped. A runny yolk will feel very delicate and will ripple beneath your finger, a partly set yolk will have a slight resistance, and a fully set yolk will feel firm.

To fry multiple eggs, follow the same method, using a pan large enough that the eggs can fit comfortably without touching and enough butter so that the pan's entire surface is lightly coated. Crack each egg into a ramekin and slide them into the pan one at a time.

poached, Makes 1 egg

1 tablespoon distilled white vinegar
1 cold egg

Fill a small saucepan halfway with water and add the vinegar. Bring to a slow simmer over medium heat, then reduce the heat to low. Crack the egg into a ramekin. Using a wooden spoon, gently swirl the water so it creates a whirlpool. Count to five before carefully sliding the egg into the middle of the swirling water. Cook for 4 to 5 minutes, making sure that the water temperature stays low enough that bubbles do not break on the surface. Carefully remove the egg using a slotted spoon and set on a paper towel to remove excess water.

To poach multiple eggs, use a large, shallow saucepan, and follow the same method, skipping the whirlpool step. Crack each egg into a ramekin and gently slide them into the water one at a time, spacing them far enough apart that they do not stick to one another.

boiled, Makes 1 egg

1 egg

Bring a small saucepan of water to boil over high heat. Using a slotted spoon or tongs, carefully lower the egg into the boiling water and cook until it has reached the desired doneness, as referenced in the chart on the right. Gently remove the egg and run under cold water to peel.

Egg boiling times:

soft | runny yolk
4 to 5 minutes

medium | partly set yolk
6 to 8 minutes

hard | fully cooked yolk
9 to 10 minutes

To boil multiple eggs, follow the same method, using a saucepan large enough to hold the eggs in one layer without crowding.

Garlic Confit

thyme
lemon peel

Makes 1 quart (1 L)

The foundation of many of our dishes has an aromatic base, consisting of herbs and garlic as the building blocks of flavor. This garlic confit takes a bit of preparation, but it will keep in your refrigerator for weeks and will become an invaluable daily tool. It can be used in place of garlic in any recipe and adds smoky, roasted notes for a bit more complexity. We also love cooking with the garlic oil itself, and using it on salads, toasts, and pastas.

1 lemon
7 heads garlic, cloves separated and peeled
2 sprigs fresh thyme
3 cups (720 ml) olive oil, plus more if needed

Preheat the oven to 250°F (120°C).

Using a vegetable peeler, remove all the yellow peel from the lemon, avoiding the bitter white pith. Drop the peels into a small ovenproof baking dish and add the garlic and thyme. Pour the olive oil over to cover, adding more as needed to fully submerge the garlic. Cover and bake until the garlic cloves are golden and tender, about 2 hours.

Remove from the oven, uncover, and let cool. Transfer the garlic and oil to a sealed container and refrigerate until ready to use.

Storage – *Refrigerate in a sealed container for up to 2 to 3 weeks.*

Basic Vegetable Stock

Makes 2 quarts (2 L)

Making a homemade stock is a great way to infuse flavors and seasonings into many of your dishes and soups. We like to keep a few pints in the freezer and defrost them as needed. A nice, light, flavorful vegetable version is great for the warmer months of spring and summer. Feel free to use any combination of vegetables and herbs you may have in your refrigerator.

1 tablespoon olive oil
2 onions, quartered
1 carrot, halved
1 fennel bulb, quartered
5 white mushrooms, halved or quartered
4 or 5 sprigs fresh thyme
2 bay leaves
1 small bunch parsley
1 teaspoon whole peppercorns
1 leek, coarsely chopped and well washed
5 garlic cloves, smashed

Heat the olive oil in a large stockpot over medium-high heat. Add all the ingredients and cook, stirring occasionally, until the vegetables begin to soften but don't yet brown, 5 to 7 minutes. Add 4 quarts (3.8 L) cold water and bring to a boil. Reduce the heat to low and simmer until the stock has reduced by half, 1 to 1½ hours. Strain the liquid, discarding the solids, and transfer the stock to storage jars.

Storage – *Refrigerate in sealed containers for 3 to 4 days or freeze for up to 1 year.*

Pickles

Makes 1 pint (480 ml)

Ideas for ingredients to pickle*

fruit
grape / apple / peach / blackberry / Anjou or Seckel
pear / nectarine / elderberry / cherry / rhubarb /
apricot / plum / husk cherry / bayberry / gooseberry /
huckleberry / wild strawberry

vegetable
green tomato / cucumber / cabbage / fennel / poblano
pepper / carrot / cauliflower / green bean / mushroom /
turnip / chile pepper / beet / corn / radish / shallot /
pearl onion / ramp / spring onion

other
golden raisin / currant / watermelon rind / edible
flower / chive blossom

* The above fruits and vegetables can be sliced, diced, or left
  whole, depending on personal preference.

We are constantly pickling, and there is (almost) no limit to what one can pickle. This basic brine can be used to quick-pickle fresh fruits, vegetables, and other items, like raisins and currants. Our refrigerator is always stocked with a few pickled items, and they add an easy crunch, color, and acidity to any dish: salads, sandwiches, toasts, eggs, etc. We've also included a list of all the items we love to pickle using this basic brine, plus a few minor variations. You can certainly add other spices, herbs, and peppercorns to the pickling liquid for extra flavor. Experiment and find your own way. This recipe will make enough brine to pickle 1 cup (240 ml) of the food of your choice. If you'd like to pickle a larger quantity, simply double (or triple) the brine ingredients and prepare as directed. Just ensure that the ingredient to be pickled is properly covered in the brine.

1½ cups (360 ml) white wine vinegar
¼ cup (50 g) sugar
½ teaspoon kosher salt
1 bay leaf
1 teaspoon whole black peppercorns
1 teaspoon mustard seeds
1 teaspoon coriander seeds
1 cup (240 ml) fruit, vegetable, or other item to be pickled (see left)

Combine the vinegar, ½ cup (120 ml) water, sugar, salt, bay leaf, peppercorns, mustard seeds, and coriander seeds in a 2-quart (2-L) saucepan and bring to a boil. Reduce the heat to low; cover and simmer for about 20 minutes.

Pack the item to be pickled into a clean quart-sized (960-ml) jar. Pour the brine into the jar and let cool. Cover and refrigerate for at least 2 hours, stirring gently once or twice.

Storage – *Refrigerate in a sealed jar for up to 1 month.*

Pickled Red Onion

Makes 1 cup (240 ml)

We use these pink pickles liberally. They are traditionally meant for tacos but are equally good on avocado toast, in salads, and even on soups.

1¼ cups (300 ml) distilled white vinegar
Juice of 2 limes
1 bay leaf
1 teaspoon fine sea salt
¼ cup (50 g) sugar
1 large red onion, thinly sliced

In a small saucepan, combine all the ingredients except the onion and bring to a simmer over low heat. Place the onion in a large bowl and carefully pour the brine over the onion. Let cool, then transfer to a clean pint-sized (480-ml) jar; cover and refrigerate.

Storage – *Refrigerate in a sealed jar for up to 1 month.*

Pickled Mustard Seeds

Makes approximately 2 cups (480 ml)

These little pops of pickle are a beautiful topping for salads and sandwiches; their tangy crunch adds a little bit of surprise to the dish.

1 cup (160 g) mustard seeds
1 bay leaf
2 cups (480 ml) white wine vinegar
½ cup (100 g) sugar
1 tablespoon kosher salt

In a small saucepan, combine all the ingredients and ¾ cup (180 ml) water and bring to a simmer over low heat. Cook until the seeds are plump and tender, about 1 hour. If too much liquid evaporates, add water as needed to keep the seeds completely covered. Let cool, then transfer to a clean pint-sized (480-ml) jar; cover and refrigerate.

Storage – *Refrigerate in a sealed jar for up to 1 month.*

Breakfast

Breakfast, celebrated as the most important meal of the day, can vary so much in approach. Some days a bowl of yogurt or oats will do; others call for a heftier affair. Taking the time to start your day with self-care and nourishment is a wonderful ritual. We are constantly inspired by ingredients, colorful foods, and beautiful, clean flavors to create morning meals for all kinds of days. Some of these are simple breakfasts for one, while others will serve a small crowd— just multiply (or divide) as needed.

Poached Eggs

black quinoa
toasted buckwheat
kefir
fermented kraut
pepita

Serves 1

Market Variations
To make the market variations, replace the underlined ingredients with the items listed below. For more detail, see page 174.

Variation 1
white quinoa / puffed amaranth / yogurt / pickled onion / black sesame

Variation 2
farro / puffed millet / crème fraîche / avocado / hazelnut

Simple, healthful, and protein-rich, this dish is a great way to start the day. It also works well as a light lunch. We often have a cooked grain at the ready in our refrigerator, making the assembly even easier during the week. We use a local brand of fermented kraut that we love, but you can also use a homemade one.

¼ cup (40 g) uncooked buckwheat
¼ cup (60 ml) kefir
½ cup (100 g) cooked black quinoa (page 25)
¼ cup (25 g) fermented kraut
2 eggs, poached (page 26)
2 tablespoons pepitas (pumpkin seeds)

Preheat the oven to 350°F (175°C).

Arrange the buckwheat in a single layer on a rimmed baking sheet and toast in the oven until lightly golden and fragrant, 6 to 8 minutes. Remove from the oven and let cool.

Pour the kefir into a shallow bowl. Spoon the quinoa and kraut along the sides of the bowl and arrange the eggs on top. Top with the toasted buckwheat and pepitas.

Fruit Salad

cantaloupe
rainier cherry
golden raspberry
ricotta

Serves 1

Market Variations
To make the market variations, replace the underlined
ingredients with the items listed below. For more detail,
see page 174.

Variation 1
plum / fig / pine berry

Variation 2
honeydew melon / boysenberry / gooseberry

Variation 3
watermelon / strawberry / apple

**Quickly assembled, this fruit plate is light
and refreshing for a warm day. Inspired
by color and season, we create this plate
on a weekday morning or a larger version
for guests for a weekend brunch. The
combination is refined, meant to enhance the
natural flavors of each element.**

1 wedge cantaloupe
½ cup (75 g) rainier cherries
¼ cup (30 g) golden raspberries
¼ cup (60 g) ricotta, good-quality store-bought or homemade (page 166)
2 teaspoons raw honey

Arrange the cantaloupe, cherries and raspberries on a plate and spoon the
ricotta on the side. Top the ricotta with a drizzle of honey.

Green Shakshuka

<u>wild greens</u>
<u>leek</u>
za'atar oil
yogurt

Serves 2 to 4

Market Variations
To make the market variations, replace the underlined ingredients with the items listed below. For more detail, see page 174.

Variation 1
green cabbage / spring onion

Variation 2
young spinach / ramp

Variation 3
dandelion greens / red onion

Traditionally, shakshuka is made with stewed tomatoes, peppers, and poached eggs. Many cultures have a version of this dish, and these days, there are many varieties of shakshuka out there. We think this one celebrates the greens of the season with bright and clean flavor profiles. It's quick to make, and we recommend serving it to a hungry few, with a good amount of fresh crusty bread alongside.

1 tablespoon unsalted butter
4 tablespoons (60 ml) olive oil
2 <u>leeks</u>, white and pale green parts only, chopped
1 Garlic Confit clove (page 28)
12 ounces (340 g) <u>wild greens</u>
Sea salt
1½ teaspoons fresh lemon juice
4 eggs
1 teaspoon za'atar
½ cup (165 ml) plain Greek yogurt

Preheat oven to 300°F (150°C).

Heat a 10-inch (25-cm) cast-iron skillet over medium heat. Add the butter and 2 tablespoons of the olive oil. When the butter has melted and just starts to bubble, add the <u>leeks</u> and reduce the heat to low. Cook, stirring occasionally, until the <u>leeks</u> are soft, about 10 minutes. Add the garlic and sauté for about 1 minute, or until fragrant. Add the <u>greens</u> and season with salt. Raise the heat to medium-high and cook, turning frequently, until wilted, 4 to 5 minutes. Add the lemon juice.

Make four indentations in the center of your <u>greens</u>. Carefully break an egg into each indentation. Transfer to the oven and bake until the egg whites are set, 12 to 14 minutes.

Meanwhile, in a small bowl, stir together the remaining 2 tablespoons olive oil and the za'atar.

To serve, scoop one egg with some of the <u>greens</u> onto each plate, top with a dollop of yogurt, and drizzle with za'atar oil.

breakfast

Breakfast Board

salmon
trout
whitefish roe
crème fraîche
sumac red onion

Serves 4 to 6

Market Variations
To make the market variations, replace the underlined ingredients with the items listed below. For more detail, see page 174.

Variation 1
smoked sable / smoked whitefish / salmon roe

Variation 2
gravlax / peppered mackerel / trout roe

A good breakfast board is perfect for a weekend gathering. It is fast to prepare and provides a myriad of flavors and combinations for guests; the possibilities are almost endless. Here you will find our favorite selections; add fresh breads or bagels from a local baker to complete the meal. Serve a fresh-brewed coffee and linger.

¼ pound (115 g) Norwegian smoked salmon
¼ pound (115 g) smoked trout
1 ounce (28 g) whitefish roe
Assorted bagels, sliced
2 tablespoons crème fraîche, good-quality store-bought or homemade (page 164)
1 tablespoon cream cheese
Cyprus flake salt
½ red onion, thinly sliced
¼ teaspoon ground sumac

Arrange the salmon and trout on a board or platter. Fill a ramekin with the roe and set it alongside the fish. Serve the bagels on a board or in a bowl.

In a small bowl, whisk together the crème fraîche and cream cheese. Transfer to a small serving bowl and top with the flaky salt. In another small bowl, toss the onion with the sumac until completely coated.

Serve the crème fraîche mixture and the sumac red onion alongside the fish and bagels.

There are many accompaniments you can add to your breakfast board. Here are some of our suggestions:

Grated horseradish / Pickled Red Onion (page 32) / caperberries / caviar / lemon zest / Cured Eggs (page 142) / Pickled Mustard Seeds (page 32) / sliced cucumber / sliced radishes / sliced tomatoes

Buttered Eggs

rye
pecorino
lemon

Serves 1

Market Variations
*To make the market variations, replace the underlined
ingredients with the items listed below. For more detail,
see page 174.*

Variation 1
sourdough / manchego

Variation 2
buckwheat / parmesan

This dish, passed down from a friend, is a simple, quick take on a warm egg salad. Look to make your eggs soft and a tad runny—soft enough to mash perfectly. You can also add the same amount of olive oil in place of the butter, if preferred. As with all our recipes, choosing the best-quality ingredients is imperative; we highly recommend a grass-fed butter and farm-fresh eggs. The result is a preparation that you will make over and over.

2 eggs
1 tablespoon salted butter
Cyprus flake salt
2 slices black rye bread (or homemade, page 22)
1 teaspoon olive oil
Grated Pecorino cheese
Zest of ½ lemon

Bring a small saucepan of water to boil over high heat. Using a slotted spoon or tongs, carefully lower the eggs into the boiling water and cook for 6 to 7 minutes. Gently remove the eggs and run under cold water to peel.

Transfer peeled eggs to a small, shallow bowl and add the butter. Mash with a fork and season with flaky salt.

Meanwhile, heat a grill to high or a grill pan over high heat. Lightly brush the bread with the olive oil and grill for 1 to 2 minutes on each side.

Spread the mashed eggs on the bread and top evenly with the Pecorino and lemon zest. Sprinkle with flaky salt before serving.

Soft-Boiled Eggs

labneh
breakfast radish
pine nut

Serves 2

Market Variations
To make the market variations, replace the underlined ingredients with the items listed below. For more detail, see page 174.

Variation 1
mascarpone / black radish / hazelnut

Variation 2
crème fraîche / purple radish / almond

Variation 3
yogurt / red radish / dukkah

This is a take on "eggs and soldiers," a British dish in which toast is served in long strips to dip into the runny egg. It is perfect for a simple breakfast and very fun if you have little ones at the table. We use breakfast radishes, but you could skip them or use any radish available at the market interchangeably.

2 eggs
2 slices ciabatta or sourdough bread
1 tablespoon olive oil
Sea salt
1 tablespoon Marinated Labneh (page 168)
½ cup (60 g) breakfast radishes, trimmed and halved
2 teaspoons pine nuts, toasted

Bring a medium saucepan of water to to a boil over high heat. Using a slotted spoon or tongs, carefully lower the eggs into the boiling water and boil for 4 to 5 minutes. Gently remove the eggs from the water and transfer to a bowl of cold water to let cool slightly.

Meanwhile, heat a grill to medium-high or a grill pan over medium-high heat. Brush both sides of the bread with the olive oil. Grill for 1 to 2 minutes. (Alternatively, simply toast the bread in a toaster oven.)

Tap and peel off the tops of the eggs using the back of a spoon and serve each in an eggcup. Sprinkle with sea salt. Top the toast with the labneh, radishes, pine nuts, and a sprinkle of sea salt. The toast can be sliced into thin strips or hand-torn for dipping into the eggs.

Slow-Cooked Oat Porridge

honeycomb
white sesame
chamomile
cyprus salt

Serves 2 to 4

Market Variations
To make the market variations, replace the underlined ingredients with the items listed below. For more detail, see page 174.

Variation 1
black sesame / currant / black salt

Variation 2
pistachio / rose / pink salt

This warm, fragrant bowl transitions us from colder days into springtime. Made creamy (and dairy-free) with a good-quality coconut milk and topped with the perfect combination of texture, sweetness, salt, and richness, each bite is inspired.

For the oats
1 cup (90 g) rolled oats
1 (13.5-ounce / 385-g) can unsweetened full-fat coconut milk
Pinch of Sonoma sea salt

For the topping
2 tablespoons unsalted butter, cut into 2 to 4 pieces
1 square of honeycomb, cut into 2 to 4 pieces
1 teaspoon white sesame seeds
1 teaspoon chamomile flowers, fresh or dried
1 teaspoon pure maple syrup
¼ teaspoon Cyprus flake salt

For the oats: In a medium saucepan, combine the oats, coconut milk, sea salt, and 1⅔ cups (400 ml) water and bring to a light boil over medium-high heat. Reduce the heat to low and simmer, stirring often, for 10 to 15 minutes, until desired thickness is achieved. Remove from the heat and let cool slightly.

For the topping: Divide the oats among two to four bowls. Divide the butter, honeycomb, sesame seeds, and chamomile evenly among the bowls. Drizzle each with the maple syrup and garnish with the flaky salt.

Smoothie Bowl

<u>espresso</u>
<u>maca</u>
<u>cinnamon</u>
<u>maple</u>
<u>banana</u>
<u>almond milk</u>

topping:
<u>hazelnut</u>
<u>cocoa nib</u>
sea salt

Serves 1

Market Variations
To make the market variations, replace the underlined ingredients with the items listed below. For more detail, see page 174.

Variation 1 – white
greek yogurt / date / banana / vanilla bean / cardamom / cashew milk
topping: puffed millet, hemp

Variation 2 – tea
rooibos / banana / date / coconut milk / honey
topping: puffed amaranth, rooibos

Variation 3 – fruit
kefir / cherry / vanilla bean / fig
topping: black sesame seed, cherry, honey

This is a nice refresher to the standard strawberry-banana smoothie, utilizing a few varied ingredients. The nuanced flavor profiles will have you charmed and invigorated. The cherry version is a house favorite and is great for little ones. Serve the smoothie in a bowl or a cup.

½ cup (120 ml) <u>unsweetened almond milk</u>
1 <u>banana</u>, frozen
1 tablespoon freshly ground <u>espresso powder</u>
1 teaspoon <u>maca powder</u>
1 teaspoon ground <u>cinnamon</u>
1 tablespoon pure <u>maple syrup</u>
2 tablespoons <u>hazelnuts</u>, toasted and halved

For the topping
1 teaspoon <u>cocoa nibs</u>
1 teaspoon fine sea salt

In a high-powered blender, combine the <u>almond milk</u>, <u>banana</u>, <u>espresso</u>, <u>maca</u>, <u>cinnamon</u>, and <u>maple syrup</u> until smooth. Pour into a bowl and garnish with the <u>hazelnuts</u>, <u>cocoa nibs</u>, and sea salt.

Toast and Roasted Fruit Jam

blueberry
balsamic
basil

Serves 1

Market Variations
To make the market variations, replace the underlined ingredients with the items listed below. For more detail, see page 175.

Variation 1
blackberry / red wine vinegar / tarragon

Variation 2
red gooseberry / white wine vinegar / thyme

This is a quick jam to make and enjoy warm. You may refrigerate it and save it for a week in an airtight jar, but be sure to reheat it for ultimate enjoyment. Adding butter to a jam is nontraditional, but makes it creamy and delightful—a perfect pairing with the tart and sweet notes of the fruit jam. Here, we serve it with an Italian buffalo butter, which is made with the unused cream from the production of mozzarella di bufala. It adds a pale and silky hue and uniquely fragrant flavor to the toast. One can, of course, substitute with any good-quality butter here.

For the jam
4 cups (680 g) fresh blueberries
2½ tablespoons sugar
2 teaspoons balsamic vinegar
1 sprig fresh basil
2 tablespoons unsalted butter

For the toast
1 slice Pullman or French bread
1 tablespoon olive oil
1 tablespoon buffalo butter, plus more for topping, if desired

For the jam: Preheat oven to 400°F (205°C).

In a small cast-iron pan, gently toss together all of the jam ingredients and transfer to the oven. Roast until the blueberries are starting to burst and the mixture is bubbling, about 15 minutes.

Remove from the oven, and place carefully on the stovetop. Cook over medium heat, stirring frequently, until the jam is thickened and syrupy, 5 to 7 minutes longer. If you find the jam to be too thick at this point, you may add a small amount of water to loosen the mixture. Remove and discard the sprig of basil.

For the toast: Heat a grill to medium-high or a grill pan over medium-high heat. Brush the bread with the olive oil on both sides and toast for about 2 minutes per side, or until golden brown. (Alternatively, you can toast the bread in the preheated oven for about 2 minutes per side.)

Spread the butter over the toast and top with a generous smear of still-warm jam. Add a dollop of butter atop the warm jam if desired.

Wilted Flower Yogurt Bowl

<u>petals</u>
<u>pistachio</u>
<u>black sesame</u>
<u>maple</u>

Serves 1

Market Variations
To make the market variations, replace the underlined ingredients with the items listed below. For more detail, see page 175.

Variation 1
chamomile / almond / white sesame / honey

Variation 2
rose / macadamia / poppy / agave

Variation 3
apple blossom / walnut / bee pollen / date syrup

We tend to always keep some edible flowers on hand to brighten any classic dish like oats and sandwiches. There are so many different varietals, and you can really use any here. Cornflowers, violets, rose petals, and nasturtium are some of our favorites. Some florals will keep longer than expected, but we find beauty in them as they wilt; the colors become more muted and the flavors a bit more enhanced. This version calls for wilted flowers; if you do not have fresh edible flowers, substitute with a dried variety. If you use fresh petals, make sure they are organic and free of all pesticides. The floral notes heighten a day-to-day dish well and add a little whimsy to a quick, wholesome breakfast.

½ cup (120 ml) yogurt, good-quality store-bought or homemade (page 164)
1 teaspoon wilted <u>edible flower petals</u>
1 tablespoon <u>pistachios</u>, coarsely chopped
1 teaspoon <u>black sesame seeds</u>
1 teaspoon pure <u>dark maple syrup</u>

Spoon the yogurt into a bowl and top with the <u>flower petals</u>, <u>pistachios</u>, and <u>sesame seeds</u>. Drizzle with the <u>maple syrup</u> to finish.

Buckwheat Bread

whipped ricotta
<u>rose</u> honey

Serves 1

Market Variations
To make the market variations, replace the underlined ingredients with the items listed below. For more detail, see page 175.

Variation 1
sprouted sourdough / chamomile honey

Variation 2
walnut loaf / cornflower honey

This meal is both beautiful and enriching to the body, making for a wonderful light start to the day. Buckwheat bread is high in protein, fiber, and nutrients. The rose honey adds beauty and fragrance to this dish. If you use fresh rose petals, make sure they are organic and free of all pesticides. Roses are also highly beneficial as a stress and inflammation reducer and are high in vitamin C and other vitamins. In Ayurvedic medicine, roses are believed to be highly beneficial and supportive for the body and mind. Be sure to use a raw local honey for added immune support.

For the <u>rose</u> honey
1 cup (240 ml) raw honey
¼ cup (10 g) fresh <u>rose petals</u>, or 2 tablespoons dried, chopped

For the whipped ricotta
1 cup (245 g) ricotta cheese, good-quality store-bought or homemade
  (page 166)
3 tablespoons whole milk or cream

For the toast
1 slice <u>buckwheat</u> bread
1 tablespoon olive oil
Peruvian pink salt
Cyprus flake salt

For the <u>rose</u> honey: In a glass jar, gently mix together the honey and <u>rose petals</u>. Cover and store at room temperature until ready to use. While the <u>rose</u> honey can be used right after it's made, it will become even better as the <u>rose petals</u> have time to infuse the honey. It will be at its most flavorful after about 2 weeks.

For the whipped ricotta: In the bowl of a stand mixer fitted with the whisk attachment, beat together the ricotta and milk on medium-high speed until light and airy.

For the toast: Heat a grill to medium-high or a grill pan over medium-high heat, or preheat the oven to 400°F (205°C). Brush the <u>bread</u> with the olive oil and toast on the grill or in the oven for about 2 minutes on each side, until lightly brown. Let cool slightly.

Spread 2 tablespoons of the whipped ricotta over the toasted bread and drizzle with 1 tablespoon of the <u>rose</u> honey. Top with a light sprinkling of pink salt and flaky salt to finish.

Storage – *The leftover ricotta will keep refrigerated for 1 to 2 days and the honey will keep for a few months in a sealed container at room temperature.*

Ricotta Pancakes

blackberry
thyme
crème fraîche
hazelnut

Serves 4 to 6

Market Variations
To make the market variations, replace the underlined ingredients with the items listed below. For more detail, see page 175.

Variation 1
rhubarb / mint / walnut

Variation 2
grape / basil / almond

These pancakes are a tried-and-true recipe for us. We love them a tad crispy on the outside, creamy and soft on the inside. The accompanying flavors are all the fun, adding sweet and salty components, plus an unexpected herb. Use plenty of butter on your pan and make stacks of these for family and friends.

For the pancakes
1½ cups (210 g) all-purpose flour
½ cup (100 g) superfine sugar
4 eggs, separated
1½ cups (360 ml) buttermilk
1 cup (245 g) ricotta, good-quality store-bought or homemade (page 166)
1 teaspoon pure vanilla extract
2 teaspoons baking powder
¼ teaspoon fine sea salt
Butter, for greasing the pan

For the blackberries
1 tablespoon unsalted butter
1 cup (155 g) blackberries
1½ tablespoons saba
2 sprigs fresh thyme
2 teaspoons honey

½ cup (120 ml) crème fraîche, good-quality store-bought or homemade (page 164)
¼ cup (35 g) hazelnuts, toasted and chopped
1 sprig fresh thyme, leaves removed and chopped

Preheat the oven to 200°F (90°C).

For the pancakes: In a large bowl, whisk together the flour, sugar, egg yolks, buttermilk, ricotta, vanilla, baking powder, and salt until well combined and smooth. In the bowl of a stand mixer fitted with the whisk attachment, or in a separate bowl using a hand mixer, whip the egg whites until they form stiff peaks. Gently fold the whipped egg whites into the batter. Set aside to rest for 5 to 10 minutes.

Meanwhile, for the blackberries: In a small sauté pan, melt the butter over medium heat. Add the blackberries, saba, and thyme sprigs and cook, tossing frequently, until the blackberries have softened and released some of their juices. Remove from the heat, discard the thyme sprigs, and stir in the honey and cover to keep warm.

Lightly grease a large nonstick griddle with butter and set over medium-low heat. Working in batches, spoon 2 tablespoons of the batter for each pancake onto the griddle. Cook until small bubbles rise to the surface of each pancake, 3 to 4 minutes. Flip the pancakes and continue to cook until golden, 3 to 4 minutes more. Transfer the pancakes to a baking sheet. Keep warm in the oven while you make the remaining pancakes.

Serve the pancakes topped with the blackberries, a dollop of crème fraîche, and a sprinkling of hazelnuts and thyme leaves.

Toasts

Assembled with ease, toasts are one of our favorite meals for all times of day. Some heartier options can be served for lunch or dinnertime, while lighter things like avocado toast are all-time favorites and sure to please. We love creating a simple toast with colorful toppings. We also love putting an unexpected item like poached salmon on bread to elevate things a bit and make a meal more filling. Toasts are good for one or two— but they are also a great dish for a gathering.

Avocado Toast

watermelon radish
mustard seed
pickled red onion
pink salt

Serves 1

Market Variations
To make the market variations, replace the underlined ingredients with the items listed below. For more detail, see page 176.

Variation 1
green tomato / pickled spring onion / cumin / cilantro / black salt

Variation 2
chive blossom / chive / fennel frond / cyprus salt

The ever-popular avocado toast is a staple for a reason. Here, we embellish it with a few seasonal elements for color and texture. Be playful: It is the combination of crunch, tartness, and salt that makes an avocado stand up to the hype. One can always add a poached egg to make this an even heftier affair.

2 slices Pullman bread (or other fresh bread of choice)
1 tablespoon olive oil, plus more for drizzling
1 avocado, sliced
Juice of ¼ lime
1 small watermelon radish, thinly sliced
2 tablespoons Pickled Red Onion (page 32)
1 teaspoon Pickled Mustard Seeds (page 32)
Peruvian pink salt

Heat a grill to medium-high or a grill pan over medium-high heat, or preheat an oven to 400°F (205°C). Brush the bread with the olive oil on both sides and toast on the grill or in the oven for about 2 minutes per side, or until golden brown.

Top the toast with slices of avocado and gently mash with a fork, if desired, to distribute evenly. Squeeze the lime juice over the avocado and arrange slices of watermelon radish and pickled red onion over top. Sprinkle with the mustard seeds and salt to taste. Drizzle with additional olive oil.

Mushroom Toast

beech
thyme
sancerre

Serves 2

Market Variations
To make the market variations, replace the underlined ingredients with the items listed below. For more detail, see page 176.

Variation 1
porcini / rosemary / pinot noir

Variation 2
blue foot / shiso / mirin

Variation 3
oyster / parsley / sherry

Variation 4
chanterelle / tarragon / chardonnay

This mushroom toast is not for the faint of heart. It is to be eaten with a knife and fork, and it can also serve as an entrée course. We love this for dinner parties, as it is simple and impressive for a crowd. Feel free to play around with different mushroom variations as they appear at your local market; they are all interchangeable.

2 thick slices sourdough bread
3 tablespoons olive oil, plus more for drizzling
2 garlic cloves, halved, or 2 Garlic Confit cloves (page 28)
1 tablespoon salted butter
2 bunches beech mushrooms, separated
2 or 3 sprigs thyme, leaves removed and chopped
½ cup (120 ml) Sancerre wine
1 cup (240 ml) heavy cream
2 tablespoons crème fraîche, good-quality store-bought or homemade (page 164)
Sea salt and freshly ground black pepper
Lemon zest
1 teaspoon truffle oil
Cyprus flake salt

Heat a grill to high or a grill pan over high heat. Brush the bread with 2 tablespoons of the olive oil and grill for 2 to 3 minutes on each side. (Alternatively, toast the bread in a preheated 400°F/205°C oven for 5 minutes, until crisp.) Rub the toast with ½ of a garlic clove for flavor.

In a medium skillet, heat the butter and remaining 1 tablespoon olive oil. Add the remaining garlic, the mushrooms, and most of the thyme and sauté for about 5 minutes. Add the Sancerre and cook for 2 to 3 minutes, until it has reduced. Add the cream and cook, stirring frequently, for 2 to 3 minutes more. Remove from the heat. Stir in the crème fraîche right before serving and season with salt and pepper.

Top each piece of toast with some of the mushrooms and a bit of sauce. Garnish with lemon zest, the truffle oil, the remaining thyme, and flaky salt.

Ramp Toast

ramp butter
roasted ramp

Serves 2

Market Variations
To make the market variations, replace the underlined ingredients with the items listed below. For more detail, see page 176.

Variation 1
spring onion butter / english runner bean

Variation 2
spring garlic butter / garlic scape

Also known as wild leeks, ramps debut in the spring, for only a few weeks. Preserving these gems in an herb butter allows us to enjoy them for a longer season. The butter can be stored in the freezer for up to a year. We recommend using it on many things other than toast—it works well on pastas, steaks, and placed on top of a risotto. To clean the ramps, remove their thin outer layer and rinse thoroughly in cold water to remove dirt. Trim the roots and dry with a dish towel. As the varieties of other spring alliums hit the market, experiment with those, including spring onions, green garlic, and leeks.

For the butter
Approximately 4 cups (150 g) packed whole ramp leaves
½ pound (2 sticks / 225 g) salted butter, softened
½ teaspoon sea salt (optional and to taste)
Zest of 1 lemon

For the roasted ramps
1 bunch ramps
2 tablespoons olive oil

For the toast
4 slices sourdough bread
1 tablespoon olive oil
Cyprus flake salt

For the butter: Prepare an ice water bath in a large bowl and set aside. Bring a medium pot of water to a boil. Submerge the ramp leaves quickly in the boiling water for about 30 seconds and no longer than 1 minute. Remove the ramp leaves and place directly in the ice water bath using tongs. When cool, remove the ramp leaves, squeeze dry, and mince.

In a stand mixer, beat the softened butter, minced ramp leaves, salt (if desired), and lemon zest until thoroughly incorporated.

For the roasted ramps: Preheat the oven to 350°F (175°C). Spread the ramps on a baking sheet and toss with the olive oil; roast for about 20 minutes, or until tender and slightly caramelized.

For the toast: Heat a grill to medium-high or a grill pan over medium-high heat. Brush the bread with the olive oil and grill for 2 to 3 minutes on each side or toast in the oven for 5 to 7 minutes.

Spread each slice with a generous layer of ramp butter, top with a few roasted ramps, and sprinkle with flaky salt to taste.

Storage – *To store the butter, transfer to a piece of plastic wrap. Shape and roll the butter into a log about 6 inches (15 cm) in length. Twist the plastic wrap at the ends to seal. This can be stored in the freezer for up to 1 year.*

Pan con Tomate

roma tomato
olive oil-fried miche

Serves 2

Market Variations
To make the market variations, replace the underlined ingredients with the items listed below. For more detail, see page 176.

Variation 1
indigo rose tomato / sourdough

Variation 2
heirloom tomato / rye bread

Bread with tomato, a very simple and straightforward toast rooted in Catalan cooking, is summer at its best. Here, the quality of ingredients is integral. This toast is served simply and is a great summer starter. If you would like to add accompaniments, try serving it with olives, anchovies, Parmesan cheese, or prosciutto slices.

4 Roma tomatoes, halved horizontally
2 slices miche bread
4 tablespoons (60 ml) extra-virgin olive oil, plus more for drizzling
1 garlic clove, halved
Cyprus flake salt

Place a box grater in a large bowl. Carefully, rub the cut faces of the tomatoes over the large holes of the box grater until you reach the skins. The flesh should be grated off, while the skin remains intact in your hand. Discard the skin and season the tomato pulp with flaky salt to taste.

Brush the bread with olive oil on both sides. Preheat a cast-iron skillet on medium-high heat and add 2 tablespoons of the remaining oil. Add the bread when hot. Grill for 2 to 3 minutes on each side, until crispy.

Remove the bread from the pan and rub lightly with the garlic. Spoon the tomato mixture over the bread. Drizzle with more olive oil and season with flaky salt. Serve immediately.

Pan con Tomate – Variation 2

Eggplant Crostini – Original Ingredients

Eggplant Crostini

black garlic
<u>tahini</u>
<u>pine nut</u>
<u>pickled red onion</u>

Serves 4 to 6

Market Variations
To make the market variations, replace the underlined ingredients with the items listed below. For more detail, see page 176.

Variation 1
yogurt / sesame / beet-cured egg

Variation 2
crème fraîche / almond / pickled pearl onion

This eggplant dish is warm and bright. It works well as a starter or as a light meal, served with a side of greens. The roasting technique is inspired by a method from London-based chef Yotam Ottolenghi.

For the eggplant
3 to 4 (about 3½ pounds / 1.6 kg total) eggplants
4 tablespoons (60 ml) olive oil
½ tablespoon salt
Freshly ground black pepper

For the <u>tahini spread</u>
¾ cup (180 ml) tahini
½ garlic clove
Juice of 1 lemon
4 tablespoons (60 ml) olive oil

For the black garlic dressing
3 black garlic cloves, peeled
1 teaspoon black sesame paste
1 teaspoon pomegranate molasses
Juice of ½ lemon
½ teaspoon sumac
½ teaspoon unsweetened cocoa powder
¼ teaspoon salt
3 tablespoons olive oil

For the toast
1 loaf miche, cut into slices ½ inch (12 mm) thick
¼ cup (60 ml) olive oil
½ cup (75 g) <u>Pickled Red Onion</u> (page 32)
¼ cup (35g) <u>pine nuts</u>, toasted
¼ cup (10 g) fresh basil leaves, torn

Preheat the oven to 400°F (205°C). Cut each eggplant into half lengthwise, and cut each half into half widthwise. Cut each quarter into thirds to create thick wedges. In a large bowl, toss the wedges with the olive oil, salt, and some pepper. Arrange the wedges on two parchment-lined baking sheets and roast until golden and slightly crisp, but not dry, 35 to 40 minutes.

For the tahini spread: Combine the tahini, garlic, lemon juice, and olive oil in a food processor and blend until smooth. The mixture should be spreadable, but not overly thick. If you wish to thin your tahini, add a thin stream of up to ½ cup (120 ml) ice water to the mixture with the motor running until your desired consistency is reached. Set aside.

For the black garlic dressing: Pulse the garlic, sesame paste, molasses, lemon juice, sumac, cocoa powder, and salt in a food processor to form a paste. With the motor running, add the olive oil in a slow and steady stream until completely incorporated.

Remove the eggplant from the oven and, while still warm, gently toss it in a large bowl with the black garlic dressing until completely coated. Set it aside to let the flavors meld.

For the toast: Heat a grill to medium-high or a grill pan over medium-high heat. Brush each slice of bread with the olive oil and toast for about 2 minutes on each side, until lightly brown.

To serve, spread each piece of toast with a bit of the <u>tahini spread</u> and top with a few wedges of warm eggplant. Garnish with <u>pickled red onions</u>, a sprinkling of <u>pine nuts</u>, and basil leaves.

Poached <u>Salmon</u> Toast

herb pesto
lemon
<u>pink salt</u>

Serves 4

Market Variations
To make the market variations, replace the underlined ingredients with the items listed below. For more detail, see page 176.

Variation 1
trout / black salt

Variation 2
sea bass / smoked salt

Variation 3
cod / cyprus salt

Poaching fish is a wonderful trick to keep in your arsenal—you can do so in olive oil, white wine, lemon, water, etc. It is quick and easy—and the added bonus is it does not create an odor in your kitchen as roasting and pan-frying might. Elevating fish on toast with herbs and fresh elements makes this a wonderful lunch or weeknight dinner.

For the fish
2 tablespoons olive oil
2 (8-ounce / 225-g) <u>wild salmon fillets</u>, skin removed

For the herb pesto
1 bunch basil
1 bunch chives
1 bunch parsley
1 bunch mint
½ clove garlic
¼ cup (35 g) pine nuts, lightly toasted
Juice of 1 lemon
½ cup (120 ml) olive oil
Sea salt

For the toast
4 slices miche bread or any other crusty bread
¼ cup (60 ml) olive oil
Peruvian <u>pink salt</u> and coarsely ground black pepper
Zest of 1 lemon

For the fish: Fill a wide, shallow pan with about 2 inches (5 cm) of water and set it over high heat. Add the olive oil and bring to a light boil. Add the <u>salmon</u> and reduce the heat to medium. Cook for 8 minutes, until the <u>salmon</u> flakes when pushed with a fork (the inside should be pink and barely cooked). Remove the <u>salmon</u> and transfer to a plate.

For the herb pesto: In a food processor, combine the basil, chives, parsley, mint, garlic, pine nuts, and lemon juice (reserve the zest). With the motor running, slowly drizzle in the olive oil. Process until smooth. Taste and season with salt.

For the toast: Heat a grill to medium-high or a grill pan over medium-high heat, or preheat the oven to 400°F (205°C). Brush the bread with the olive oil and toast on the grill or in the oven for about 2 minutes on each side, until lightly brown.

Spread the herb pesto generously over the toast. Flake the still-warm <u>salmon</u> over the pesto. Season with <u>pink salt</u>, a few cracks of black pepper, and the lemon zest.

Bowls

Eating in a bowl somehow feels immediately comforting and healthful. These recipes are simple and fresh preparations—fit for one or a group. Some are lighter soups appropriate as we transition into the warmer season, and the Everyday Bowl is one we make time and time again, as it's perfect for any day and any time of the year.

Parmesan Brodo

egg
<u>young spinach</u>
<u>radish</u>

Serves 4

Market Variations
To make the market variations, replace the underlined ingredients with the items listed below. For more detail, see page 177.

Variation 1
mustard green / english pea

Variation 2
sorrel / white asparagus

A Parmesan *brodo* is a broth created from the rinds of Parmesan cheese. The result is light but simultaneously abundant in flavor and richness. Adding simple, delicate spring vegetables and an oozy egg makes a wonderful bowl of goodness. You can save your rinds in the freezer until you have enough for a broth. Be sure to use a good Italian Parmigiano-Reggiano for best results.

For the aromatic bundle
8 ounces (225 g) Parmesan cheese rinds, any paper at the ends removed
½ teaspoon whole black peppercorns
Handful of fresh flat-leaf parsley
2 or 3 sprigs fresh thyme
1 bay leaf

For the brodo
1 large onion, quartered
Sea salt
3 cups (90 g) <u>young spinach</u>
4 eggs, poached (page 26)
1 <u>radish</u>, shaved on a mandoline
8 to 10 baby turnips, greens removed
1 ounce (28 g) Parmesan cheese, shaved on a mandoline

Cyprus flake salt and coarsely ground black pepper

For the bundle: Place all the ingredients in the center of an 8-inch (20-cm) square or larger piece of cheesecloth. Bring the corners of the cheesecloth together to create a bundle and tie with a piece of kitchen twine.

For the brodo: Place the bundle in a stockpot and add 8 cups (2 L) water and the onion and bring to a boil. Reduce the heat to low and simmer for about 45 minutes, until the liquid has reduced by about half. Pour the broth through a fine-mesh strainer. You should have about 4½ cups (1 L) of broth. Return the broth to the pot over low heat and season with sea salt. Add the <u>spinach</u> and cook for 2 to 3 minutes, until wilted but still bright green. Remove from the heat.

To serve, ladle the broth and <u>greens</u> into four bowls. Top each with a poached egg, <u>radish</u>, baby turnips, and Parmesan shavings. Season with flaky salt and coarsely ground pepper.

Everyday Bowl

<u>farro</u>
<u>market radish</u>
<u>roasted purple carrot</u>
watercress dressing
<u>piave</u>

Serves 2 to 4

Market Variations
To make the market variations, replace the underlined ingredients with the items listed below. For more detail, see page 177.

Variation 1
quinoa / purple spring onion / roasted asparagus / pecorino

Variation 2
millet / lacinato kale / roasted beet / parmesan

Variation 3
bulgur / shaved fennel / roasted red pepper / manchego

We call this an everyday bowl because you should be able to make a version of this any day, with whatever you have on hand, and never get tired of it. It's a wonderful idea to keep a batch of cooked grains in the fridge so you can combine them effortlessly with something nice and fresh, some roasted vegetables, something creamy, and this perfectly tangy watercress dressing.

For the roasted <u>carrots</u>
12 purple carrots (about 455 g total), unpeeled, scrubbed
2 tablespoons olive oil
1 tablespoon white vinegar
1 tablespoon pure maple syrup
Sea salt and freshly ground black pepper

For the watercress dressing
6 cups (about 205 g) watercress leaves
1 tablespoon white wine vinegar
½ teaspoon sea salt, plus more as needed
Juice of ½ lemon
½ cup (240 ml) olive oil

1 cup (200 g) <u>farro</u>, cooked (page 25)
1 market <u>radish</u>, thinly sliced on a mandoline
2 heaping tablespoons Greek yogurt
2 Cured Eggs, halved (page 142)
1 ounce (28 g) <u>Piave</u> cheese
Avocado oil, for garnish
Sea salt and coarsely ground black pepper

Preheat the oven to 400°F (205°C). Line a baking sheet with parchment paper.

For the carrots: Spread the carrots out on the prepared baking sheet and drizzle with the olive oil, vinegar, and maple syrup. Season with salt and pepper and roast for about 10 minutes. Give the pan a quick shake to ensure even browning, then roast for 10 minutes or so more, until the carrots are cooked through and beginning to brown.

For the dressing: Combine all the dressing ingredients in a food processor. Blend until smooth and season with more salt, if needed.

Into each bowl, scoop the desired amount of <u>farro</u> and top with <u>radish</u> and roasted <u>carrots</u>. Divide the yogurt in dollops on the side of each bowl. Add a heaping tablespoon of watercress dressing to each bowl and arrange the cured egg beside it. Top with <u>Piave</u>, drizzle with avocado oil, and season with sea salt and pepper.

White Miso Soup

<u>soba noodle</u>
<u>black trumpet mushroom</u>
<u>bok choy</u>
<u>beet-cured egg</u>

Serves 4

Market Variations
To make the market variations, replace the underlined ingredients with the items listed below. For more detail, see page 177.

Variation 1
ramen noodle / shiitake mushroom / spinach / saffron-cured egg

Variation 2
rice noodle / cremini mushroom / kale / cured egg

As the days get longer and warmer, this is a light and fragrant bowl of goodness, rich in nutrients and immunity builders that seems to signal spring. We make this pot if we're under the weather or simply having a quiet afternoon at home. Nourishing to the body and soul, this warm bowl is a staple in our home. Be sure to add the miso as directed in order to preserve the natural enzymes and ensure its utmost benefits.

8 ounces (225 g) <u>dried soba noodles</u>

For the dashi
6 cups (1.4 L) Basic Vegetable Stock (page 30) or water
1 (4-inch / 10-cm) piece kombu (dried kelp)
1 (2-inch / 5-cm) piece fresh ginger, peeled and smashed
1 garlic clove, smashed
2 bunches <u>baby bok choy</u>, separated
8 ounces (225 g) <u>black trumpet mushrooms</u>, sliced
12 ounces (340 g) firm silken tofu, cut into ½-inch (12-mm) cubes
2 tablespoons (35 g) white miso
2 <u>Beet-cured Eggs</u> (page 142), halved
Black sesame seeds, for serving
Sesame oil, for serving
Sriracha, for serving

Fill a large pot with water and bring to a boil. Add the <u>noodles</u> and cook for 3 to 4 minutes, or according to the package instructions. Drain and rinse well under cold water. Set aside in a bowl with a bit of cool water to keep the <u>noodles</u> from sticking while you prepare the dashi.

In a large pot, combine the stock, kombu, ginger, and garlic and bring to a simmer over low heat. Add the <u>bok choy</u>, <u>mushrooms</u>, and tofu and simmer just until the <u>mushrooms</u> are tender and the <u>bok choy</u> has wilted, 2 to 3 minutes. Remove the pot from the heat. Spoon one ladle of the hot dashi into a small bowl. Add the miso and whisk until thoroughly incorporated. Add the miso mixture to the pot and stir to combine.

Ladle the dashi and vegetables into serving bowls, add <u>noodles</u>, and garnish with the <u>cured eggs</u>, sesame seeds, sesame oil, and sriracha as desired.

Plates

Plates reside somewhere between a salad and a main course—assembly is your foremost concern here. The components and flavors are meant to come together in a particular way. These are fresh takes on the traditional: a panzanella, a crudo, a ceviche, and a Niçoise, which let our specially sourced ingredients shine. We serve these as hefty starters—or in their own right, they are perfect for light meals as the weather warms.

Ceviche

halibut
yellowfin tuna
red onion
kaffir lime
poblano
crispy garlic

Serves 2 to 4

Market Variations
To make the market variations, replace the underlined ingredients with the items listed below. For more detail, see page 178.

Variation 1
grouper / snapper / treviso

Variation 2
fluke / scallop / avocado

This meal transports you to the beaches of the Yucatán, one of our favorite locations. We bring this back with us for a feeling of summer and the lightest fare you can imagine on a hot summer night. This dish calls for the fish to be sliced; however, you can certainly cut it into small cubes, which is a bit more traditional for a ceviche. And as always, experiment with flavors and elements here. The main components are acid, crunch, flavor, and a fresh element. You can also add a spicy chile for a bit of heat.

1 (8-ounce / 225-g) halibut fillet
1 (8-ounce / 225-g) yellowfin tuna fillet
5 kaffir lime leaves, thinly sliced
½ cup (120 ml) lime juice (from 4 limes), plus the zest from 2 for garnish
½ cup plus 2 tablespoons (150 ml) olive oil
3 garlic cloves, thinly sliced on a mandoline
Cyprus flake salt
½ red onion, thinly sliced
½ poblano pepper, minced
¼ cup (40 g) oil-cured olives

Cut both fish against the grain into ¼-inch (6-mm) slices, working with a very sharp knife positioned at a 45-degree angle and using a fluid motion to cut. Alternatively you can cut the fish into ¼-inch (6-mm) cubes.

Transfer the fish to a medium glass bowl. Add the lime leaves, lime juice, and 2 tablespoons of the olive oil and gently toss to combine. Let sit for 3 to 5 minutes.

In a small sauté pan or cast-iron skillet, heat the remaining ½ cup (120 ml) olive oil over medium heat. Once the oil begins to shimmer, working in small batches, add the garlic slices and fry for 20 to 30 seconds, or until just lightly golden brown. Using a slotted spoon, transfer the garlic chips to a paper towel-lined plate to drain.

To serve, arrange the fish on a platter and season with flaky salt. Top with the red onion, poblano, olives, lime zest, and garlic chips.

Spring Salad

zucchini crudo
buffalo mozzarella
lemon balm
almond

Serves 2 to 4

Market Variations
To make the market variations, replace the underlined ingredients with the items listed below. For more detail, see page 178.

Variation 1
purple snow pea / red sorrel / yogurt / cilantro flower

Variation 2
fennel / pecorino / basil

Variation 3
sugar snap pea / crème fraîche / tarragon

A simple assembly, this dish requires little cooking. We love it for outdoor dinners and summer nights with friends. The long squash ribbons can sit in their marinade for up to 30 minutes, allowing them to soften but retain a bit of bite. When the market is abundant with a variety of squashes, experiment with your favorites.

2 zucchini or summer squash
1 (8-ounce / 225-g) ball buffalo mozzarella, torn into large pieces
¼ cup (10 g) whole lemon balm leaves
¼ cup (30 g) slivered almonds, lightly toasted
¼ cup (60 ml) olive oil
Zest and juice of ½ lemon
Cyprus flake salt

Using a mandoline, shave the zucchini lengthwise into long ribbons ⅛ inch (3 mm) thick. Arrange them on a serving platter and top with the mozzarella, lemon balm, and almonds. Drizzle the olive oil and lemon juice over the top, and finish with a sprinkling of lemon zest and flaky salt.

Grilled Octopus

burnt citrus crema
braised olive
parsley

Serves 2 to 4

Market Variations
To make the market variations, replace the underlined ingredients with the items listed below. For more detail, see page 178.

Variation 1
yogurt / caperberry

Variation 2
black tahini / pickled mustard seed

Variation 3
charred eggplant puree / castelvetrano olive

Grilled octopus is one of those dishes we often eat at restaurants but rarely take on at home. We encourage you to try it—it's an endeavor, but certainly not as difficult as it sounds. Once the perfect char is mastered, the moist interior and the combination of simple flavors are memorable and worthwhile. If using baby octopus, simply grill for less time, 2 to 3 minutes on each side.

For the burnt citrus crema
1 lemon
½ cup (120 ml) crème fraîche, good-quality store-bought or homemade (page 164)
½ teaspoon ground cumin
Sea salt

For the octopus
1 bay leaf
10 peppercorns
1 lemon, sliced
1 pound (455 g) cleaned octopus tentacles
Olive oil
Sea salt and freshly ground black pepper
Juice of ½ lemon
1 cup (30 g) parsley leaves
½ cup (50 g) Braised Black Olives (page 140)

For the burnt citrus crema: Slice the rind off the lemon, squaring it off, then slice the lemon in half. Heat the grill (alternatively, use a grill pan) to medium-high and place both lemon halves on the grill. Grill for 3 to 4 minutes on each side, until the lemon has a nice char to the exterior. Transfer to a chopping board and coarsely chop the lemon.

In a mixing bowl, combine the crème fraîche and the charred, chopped lemon. Fold in the cumin and season with salt. Set aside.

For the octopus: Fill a large pot halfway with water. Add the bay leaf, peppercorns, lemon, and octopus. Cover and bring to a boil over medium-high heat. Reduce the heat to medium and simmer for 30 minutes, until the octopus is tender. Transfer to a plate and set aside. Discard the water and spices.

To finish the octopus, heat a grill (or a grill pan) to high. Brush the octopus with olive oil and season with sea salt and pepper. Grill until charred, about 5 minutes on each side.

To serve, spread the burnt citrus crema over a large serving platter. Set the octopus on top and season with sea salt. Garnish with the lemon juice, parsley, and olives.

Smoked Black Bread Panzanella – Original Ingredients

Smoked Black Bread Panzanella

<u>beet</u>
<u>purple kale</u>
<u>radicchio</u>
<u>smoked ricotta</u>
saba

Serves 2 to 4

Market Variations
To make the market variations, replace the underlined ingredients with the items listed below. For more detail, see page 178.

Variation 1
carrot / mizuna / watercress / yogurt

Variation 2
tomato / arugula / purple basil / burrata

This platter is a combination of warm, smoky, sweet, and bitter. The flavors and colors speak for themselves, and the addition of smoked ricotta is remarkable. We use a variety from Salvatore Brooklyn, which can be found at boutique grocers and cheese shops. If you cannot find smoked ricotta, opt for a great-quality cow's-milk ricotta, or make your own (page 166). Saba, which is drizzled atop this salad, is our most favorite vinegar. In Italian, *saba* means "cooked grape juice," and is a sweet unfermented syrup made from the "must" of Trebbiano grapes and adds a gorgeous caramelized grape flavor and deep hue to the plate.

For the croutons
½ cup (120 ml) olive oil
1 tablespoon black sesame paste
1 tablespoon balsamic vinegar
3 to 5 garlic cloves, smashed
Cyprus flake salt
¼ loaf of miche, torn into large pieces

For the <u>beets</u>
3 or 4 large <u>beets</u>, unpeeled, scrubbed well and halved
1 or 2 baby <u>beets</u>, unpeeled, scrubbed well
3 tablespoons olive oil
1 tablespoon sherry vinegar

For the <u>kale</u>
3 or 4 leaves purple kale
2 teaspoons olive oil

For the salad
½ head <u>radicchio</u>, leaves torn
½ cup (125 g) <u>smoked ricotta</u>
2 tablespoons olive oil
2 tablespoons saba (grape must syrup)
Cyprus flake salt

Preheat the oven to 400°F (205°C). Line a rimmed baking sheet with parchment paper. In a large bowl, whisk together the olive oil, sesame paste, and vinegar. Add the garlic, flaky salt, and bread and toss. Spread the croutons in a single layer on the prepared baking sheet. Roast for 10 to 12 minutes, until crisp. Remove from the oven and let cool. Keep the oven on.

For the <u>beets</u>: In a cast-iron skillet, toss the <u>beets</u> in the olive oil and vinegar until completely coated. Transfer to the oven and roast until fork-tender and slightly crispy on the outside, 40 to 45 minutes. Remove from the oven and set aside.

For the kale: Line a baking sheet with parchment paper. Brush the kale leaves with the olive oil and arrange them on the baking sheet, making sure the leaves do not overlap. Roast until crisp, 3 to 5 minutes.

Arrange the <u>radicchio leaves</u>, <u>kale</u>, and <u>beets</u> on a platter. Top with the croutons and spoon the <u>smoked ricotta</u> on the side. Drizzle with the olive oil and saba and finish with flaky salt.

Deconstructed Niçoise Salad

market lettuce
halibut
potato
haricot vert
braised olive
soft egg

Serves 4

Market Variations
To make the market variations, replace the underlined ingredients with the items listed below. For more detail, see page 178.

Variation 1
frisée / salmon / romano bean / cornichon

Variation 2
treviso / tuna / snow pea / caper

Variation 3
mâche / cod / yellow wax bean / anchovy

This is a great dish to serve on a large platter, family-style, and is quite impressive when all the elements below are made as instructed. We make a version of this dish often, and because there are so many elements, some can easily be omitted if they are not available to you.

For the dressing
½ shallot, minced
1½ tablespoons Dijon mustard
2 tablespoons white wine vinegar
½ cup (120 ml) olive oil
½ teaspoon sea salt
Freshly ground black pepper

For the potatoes
1 pound (455 g) baby potatoes
½ cup (120 ml) olive oil
1 teaspoon mustard seeds

For the fish
¼ cup (60 ml) white wine
3 sprigs fresh thyme
1 (1-pound/455-g) halibut fillet

For the beans
4 ounces (115 g) haricot verts, trimmed
1 tablespoon salted butter

For the salad
1 head market lettuce
½ cup (75 g) Braised Black Olives (page 140, using Niçoise olives)
4 eggs, soft-boiled, halved (page 26)
Sea salt and freshly ground black pepper

For the dressing: In a large bowl, whisk together the shallot, mustard, and vinegar. While whisking, slowly drizzle in the olive oil and whisk until emulsified. Season with the salt and pepper. Leave half the dressing in the bowl and transfer the remainder to a separate small bowl.

For the potatoes: Fill a medium saucepan halfway with water. Cover and bring to a boil over medium-high heat. Add the potatoes, reduce the heat to medium-low, and cook for about 10 minutes, until the potatoes are fork-tender. Let cool, then add to the large bowl and smash with the back of a spoon. Toss with half of the dressing and mustard seeds.

For the fish: Fill a wide shallow saucepan one-quarter of the way with water. Add the wine and thyme and bring to a simmer over medium-high heat. Add the halibut and simmer until cooked through, about 3 minutes. Remove the halibut and transfer to a large platter.

For the beans: Fill a large pot one-quarter of the way with water and bring to a boil over medium-high heat. Add the haricot verts to the boiling water, blanch for 2 minutes, then drain. In a large saucepan, melt the butter over medium heat. Add the haricot verts and toss to coat with the warm butter.

Add the lettuce leaves to the large platter. Arrange the potatoes, haricot verts, and olives over the lettuce. Pour the reserved dressing evenly over the top. Add the eggs and season with salt and pepper.

Vegetables

As the seasons shift each year, we are invited to explore all our favorite vegetables in a new manner. Our approach here is fuss-free. The focus is on celebrating the produce at its best—keeping the nature and flavors of the item intact, while adding a bit of nuance and enhancement. We try to keep the integrity of the vegetable by cooking it simply and enhancing it with bold flavors like a garlic confit, cheeses, and vinegars. This chapter is less about alternates and more about the vegetables taking center stage. This way, the produce speaks for itself—in both beauty and form.

Skillet-Charred Greens

Serves 2 to 4

The simplest of preparations, this dish properly respects the integrity of the season's greens. The charring is best done in a cast-iron skillet to properly sear the greens at a very high temperature. This process allows you to sear, blanch, and crisp the greens quickly and in one pan. While we focus on broccolini, which is particularly delicious in the spring, the same approach can be taken for any hearty greens at the market, including wild greens, collards, kale, escarole, or even fiddlehead ferns.

2 tablespoons Garlic Confit oil (page 28)
3 or 4 Garlic Confit cloves (page 28)
2 bunches broccolini, larger stalks halved lengthwise
1 tablespoon olive oil
Cyprus flake salt
2 tablespoons shaved Parmesan cheese
Squeeze of lemon

Heat a cast-iron skillet over very high heat. Add the garlic confit oil and cloves.

Wash the greens and, while they're still a little wet, add them to the pan. Allow to sizzle for 2 to 3 minutes. Add ¼ cup (60 ml) water, reduce the heat to medium, cover, and steam the greens for 3 to 4 minutes. Uncover the skillet and increase the heat to high. Add the olive oil, season with salt, and add the cheese. Toss once with tongs in the skillet, then cook for 2 to 3 minutes more, until the greens are charred to your liking. Squeeze lemon juice over the top and serve.

Oxheart Tomatoes, fresh

Serves 2 to 4

At their peak, not much has to be done to tomatoes to enjoy their beautiful taste. This is a simple preparation that celebrates the inherent sweetness of the tomato. We use the Oxheart (yellow) variety here, but feel free to use any type of heirloom tomato you find at your local market.

4 Oxheart tomatoes, sliced
Cyprus flake salt
¼ cup (25 g) shaved ricotta salata
Zest of 1 lemon
¼ cup (13 g) fresh parsley, finely chopped
3 tablespoons extra-virgin olive oil

Arrange the tomatoes on a platter. Season with flaky salt, then top with the ricotta, lemon zest, and parsley. Drizzle with the olive oil immediately before serving.

Fiesole Artichokes

The beauty of baby artichokes is that they can be used whole and, therefore, require very little prep (compared to their larger relatives, globe artichokes). Artichokes can be found year-round, but peak in springtime with their best varieties. Here, they are braised with the most basic ingredients, a combination that can work with almost any hearty vegetable, like mushrooms, cauliflower, or hefty greens. Chive blossoms, part of the allium family, make a debut in the midst of summer and are a beautiful addition to dishes, adding a slight onion taste.

For the aioli
1 garlic clove
1 egg yolk
Juice of ¼ lemon, plus more as needed
¼ teaspoon fine sea salt, plus more as needed
¼ cup (60 ml) extra-virgin olive oil
¼ cup (60 ml) grapeseed oil
1 tablespoon chive blossom petals

For the artichokes
8 baby purple Fiesole artichokes
3 tablespoons extra-virgin olive oil
¼ teaspoon Cyprus flake salt
⅛ teaspoon freshly ground black pepper
¼ cup (60 ml) white wine
2 tablespoons fresh lemon juice (about ½ lemon)
2 garlic cloves, crushed
1¼ teaspoons nigella seeds

For the aioli: In a food processor, combine the garlic, egg yolk, lemon juice, and salt and process until smooth, about 30 seconds. With the motor running, add the olive oil in a slow, steady stream, then repeat with the grapeseed oil. If the aioli becomes too thick, thin it with a teaspoon of water. Transfer the aioli to a bowl and fold in the chive blossom petals. Taste and adjust the seasoning as needed with more salt and/or lemon juice.

For the artichokes: Wash the artichokes and pat them dry. Trim the ends and remove the outer leaves, then halve each artichoke.

In a nonstick skillet, heat the olive oil over medium-high heat until just shimmering. Place the artichokes cut side down in the pan in a single layer and season with the salt and pepper. Cook until the oil is bubbling and hot, and the cut sides of the artichokes have started to brown, about 3 minutes. Add the wine, lemon juice, and garlic and cook for 1 to 2 minutes more. Add 1 teaspoon of the nigella seeds, reduce the heat to low, cover, and cook until the artichokes are fork-tender, about 20 minutes. Remove from the heat and let cool slightly.

Spoon the aioli onto a serving platter and top with the artichoke halves. Garnish with the remaining ¼ teaspoon nigella seeds and season with flaky salt. Serve the artichokes warm or at room temperature.

Burnt Carrots

Serves 4

Roasting at a very high heat, these carrots become soft on the inside and crunchy on the exterior, bringing out their natural sweetness. Carrots can be found at markets year-round, but as spring approaches you'll see more beautiful heirloom varieties: purple, black, red, white, and yellow—each with subtle flavor nuances. Chervil is a delicate spring herb in the parsley family with a faint anise taste. If you cannot find chervil, it can be replaced with parsley leaves.

2½ tablespoons olive oil
2½ tablespoons pure maple syrup
¼ teaspoon Cyprus flake salt, plus more for garnish
6 bunches baby carrots (about 30 small), scrubbed
½ cup (25 g) fresh chervil leaves
2 or 3 balls of Marinated Labneh (page 168)
½ teaspoon nigella seeds
¼ cup hazelnuts, halved and toasted

Preheat the oven to 500°F (260°C). Line a baking sheet with parchment paper.

In a large bowl, stir together the olive oil, maple syrup, and salt. Add the carrots and toss to coat. Spread the carrots in a single layer on the prepared baking sheet, top with half of the chervil, and bake for 10 to 12 minutes, watching to ensure that the carrots char but do not burn too much.

Spread the labneh on a platter using the back of a spoon. Rest the carrots atop the labneh and top with the hazelnuts, remaining chervil, and nigella seeds. Season with flaky salt and serve.

Asparagus, buttered and shaved

Serves 4

It's all about texture with asparagus—allowing the spears to cook properly so that they have simultaneous bite and softness, retaining their flavor and inherent crunch. Buttering the asparagus is a timeless French method, and it works. The additional ribbons add a bit of whimsy to the plate. It's fun to use the purple variety of asparagus, when it pops up at the market. Note that cooking the purple asparagus will turn it green—but a quick blanch will still leave some color on the spear edges. The asparagus colors can of course be interchangeable, depending on what is available.

1 bunch purple asparagus, trimmed
2 tablespoons good-quality salted French butter, cut into small pieces
5 or 6 stalks white asparagus, trimmed
Squeeze of lemon juice
Cyprus flake salt

Bring a large pot of water to a boil. Add the purple asparagus and blanch for 2 to 3 minutes. Transfer immediately to a large bowl. Add the butter and toss until it has completely melted and the asparagus is nicely coated.

Using a vegetable peeler, peel the white asparagus into long ribbons.

Arrange the ribbons of white asparagus on a serving platter and top with the blanched purple asparagus. Squeeze lemon juice over the top and sprinkle with flaky salt.

Mains

Cooking in the warmer months often means a consideration of time and warmer-weather temperature. Our meals are lighter and quicker. We grill a whole fish or sausage outdoors when the weather permits. Or on days when we want to invite friends over, brisket tacos cooking slow and steady at a low heat are great for a crowd. In this chapter you will find meals for all days, in varying degrees of complexity. These dishes are meant to be hearty, robust, and beautiful to serve.

Whole Fish

yellowtail snapper
sumac red onion

Serves 4

Market Variations
To make the market variations, replace the underlined ingredients with the items listed below. For more detail, see page 179.

Variation 1
branzino / pickled fennel

Variation 2
sea bass / radish

Grilling whole fish is a summer meal at its very best. Choose wild, fresh fish, and speak to your fishmonger about what is in season in your area. This version utilizes a few common offerings during the spring and summer months. The accompaniments are straightforward, creating a beautiful and easy meal. If you have leftover sumac red onions, keep them in the refrigerator for later use on salads and sandwiches, as you would a pickle. This meal is great served outdoors and for a small group.

For the fish
2 whole yellowtail snappers, about 1½ pounds (680 g) each, cleaned
2 tablespoons olive oil
Sea salt and freshly ground black pepper
2 lemons
4 sprigs fresh thyme
4 sprigs fresh oregano

For the red onions
½ red onion, thinly sliced, preferably using a mandoline
1 tablespoon ground sumac

For the vinaigrette
¼ cup (60 ml) distilled white vinegar
Juice of ½ lemon
6 tablespoons (90 ml) olive oil
Sea salt and freshly ground black pepper
4 sprigs fresh parsley
4 sprigs fresh cilantro
4 sprigs fresh mint

For the fish: Heat a grill to high and preheat the oven to 400°F (205°C). Line a baking sheet with parchment paper.

Wash and dry the snappers. Rub them all over with 1 tablespoon of the olive oil (using about ½ tablespoon for each fish) and season with salt and pepper. Slice one of the lemons and divide the slices between the two fish, stuffing them and the thyme and oregano into the cavities.

Place the snappers on the preheated grill for about 5 minutes on each side, until the skin gets a nice char. Transfer both fish to the prepared baking sheet and bake for 10 to 15 minutes, or until the flesh is opaque and can be easily flaked with a fork. Alternatively, to roast them, place the fish on the prepared baking sheet and bake for 25 to 30 minutes.

Meanwhile, for the red onions: In a medium bowl, toss the onions with the sumac. Set aside.

For the vinaigrette: In a medium bowl, whisk together the vinegar and lemon juice. While whisking, slowly drizzle in the olive oil until emulsified. Season with salt and pepper.

Fillet the fish, transfer the fillets to a platter, and immediately pour the vinaigrette on top. Top with the red onions, parsley, cilantro, and mint.

Sausage

buttered <u>purple cabbage</u>
<u>yogurt</u>
<u>pickled mustard seed</u>
charred pearl onion

Serves 2

Market Variations
*To make the market variations, replace the underlined
ingredients with the items listed below. For more detail,
see page 179.*

Variation 1
green cabbage / labneh / pickled red onion

Variation 2
napa cabbage / burnt citrus crema / pickled fennel

Variation 3
savoy cabbage / fromage blanc / pickled radish

**This dish is an elevated backyard meal,
light and bright, but also perfectly filling.
The charred elements evoke the smokiness
of a perfect summer eve. We use a salt-
and-pepper sausage of pork and beef from
our local butcher, and recommend you
experiment with different varieties. A good-
quality sausage will make all the difference.**

2 (5-ounce / 140-g) sausages of your choice
1 cup (110 g) pearl onions, peeled
3 tablespoons olive oil
1 garlic clove, minced
½ head <u>purple cabbage</u>, cored and shredded
3 tablespoons white wine vinegar
Sea salt and freshly ground black pepper
2 tablespoons unsalted butter
2 tablespoons <u>Greek yogurt</u>
½ cup (120 g) <u>Pickled Mustard Seeds</u> (page 32)

Heat a grill to high or a grill pan over high heat. Grill the sausages for 6 to 8
minutes on each side (depending on their size), flipping once. The sausages
are ready when firm to the touch. Leave the grill on.

To peel the pearl onions: Bring a saucepan full of water to a boil, add the
onions, boil for 2 minutes, then submerge them in cold water. The peels will
come off easily.

Add the onions to the hot grill or grill pan to char, turning them frequently,
for 10 to 12 minutes, until the outer layer is darkened. If using a grill, place
onions on foil first. Remove and set aside.

In the meantime, heat the olive oil in a large skillet over medium heat.
Add the garlic and sauté for 1 to 2 minutes. Reduce the heat to low, add the
<u>cabbage</u>, and cover the pan. Cook, stirring frequently, until the <u>cabbage</u>
begins to soften, about 2 minutes. Add the vinegar and season with salt
and pepper. Add the butter and cook, covered, for 5 minutes more, until
the <u>cabbage</u> is soft but still retains some texture.

To serve, spread the <u>yogurt</u> on the bottom of a large platter and place the
<u>cabbage</u> and sausages atop. Add the charred onions and <u>mustard seeds</u>
for garnish.

Dukkah-Covered Schnitzel

baby gem lettuce
fennel
pea shoot
roasted garlic dressing

Serves 4

Market Variations
To make the market variations, replace the underlined ingredients with the items listed below. For more detail, see page 179.

Variation 1
bread crumb / romaine / cucumber / watercress

Variation 2
panko / red leaf lettuce / summer squash / chickweed

This dish is a contemporary take on a classic schnitzel. Served with a clean spring salad, it is a light and beautiful meal. Encrusting the chicken in dukkah creates a perfect crunchy exterior and lends aromatic flavor. You can experiment with different dukkah varieties (page 146) or simply go the classic bread crumb route.

For the dressing
2 egg yolks
8 to 10 Garlic Confit cloves (page 28)
1½ tablespoons white wine vinegar
2 tablespoons sherry vinegar
Juice of ½ lemon
¾ cup (180 ml) olive oil
Sea salt and freshly ground black pepper

For the schnitzel
1 cup Earth Dukkah (page 146)
½ cup (45 g) bread crumbs
¼ cup (25 g) finely grated Parmesan cheese
4 chicken cutlets, lightly pounded to ½ inch (12 mm) thick
3 tablespoons olive oil

3 heads baby gem lettuce, halved or quartered
2 cups (130 g) pea shoots
½ cup (45 g) shaved fennel (less than ½ bulb)
Chopped fresh flat-leaf parsley, for serving

For the dressing: In a food processor, combine the egg yolks, garlic, vinegars, and lemon juice and pulse to combine. With the motor running, slowly add the olive oil in a steady stream. Season with salt and pepper. Pour half the dressing into a wide, shallow bowl. Pour the remainder into a separate small bowl and set aside.

For the schnitzel: Preheat the oven to 425°F (220°C). Line a baking sheet with parchment paper.

In a wide, shallow bowl, combine the dukkah with the bread crumbs and Parmesan. Set the shallow bowl of dressing nearby. Working one at a time, dip each cutlet into the dressing until completely coated. Let the excess dressing drip off, then dredge the cutlet in the dukkah mixture, making sure both sides are evenly coated. (Discard the dressing you used for the cutlets.)

Arrange the coated cutlets on the prepared baking sheet and drizzle with the olive oil on both sides. Bake for 20 minutes. Remove from the oven and carefully flip each cutlet. Return to the oven and bake until the cutlets are evenly golden and cooked through, about 5 minutes more.

Spread a bit of the reserved dressing on a platter and top with the lettuce, pea shoots, and fennel. Add the chicken cutlets and sprinkle with the parsley. Serve with the reserved dressing on the side.

Brisket Tacos

napa cabbage
pickled red onion
cotija

Serves 4 to 6

Market Variations
To make the market variations, replace the underlined ingredients with the items listed below. For more detail, see page 179.

Variation 1
purple cabbage / pickled radish / queso fresco

Variation 2
summer corn / pickled poblano / queso blanco

This meal brings great joy to our family. It does take time to braise, slow and steady, to create a tender and flavorful result. If you happen to own a slow cooker, you can certainly use it for this. Otherwise, use a good cast-iron casserole or Dutch oven. We love finding homemade tortillas, even if it means ordering plain ones from a local Mexican restaurant.

1 (3- to 4-pound / 1.4- to 1.8-kg) first-cut beef brisket
Kosher salt and freshly ground black pepper
2 tablespoons (30 g) olive oil
1 red onion, quartered
8 garlic cloves or Garlic Confit cloves (page 28)
¼ cup (60 ml) red wine vinegar
4 cups (960 ml) beef broth
1 cup (165 g) crushed tomatoes
2 tablespoons tomato paste
½ teaspoon ground cumin
1 teaspoon smoked paprika
½ teaspoon ground coriander
½ cup (20 g) chopped fresh cilantro leaves, plus more for garnish
1 bay leaf

For serving
¾ cup (180 ml) sour cream
1 tablespoon fresh lime juice
¼ teaspoon sea salt
8 to 12 corn tortillas
2 cups (140 g) shredded napa cabbage
1 cup Pickled Red Onion (page 32)
½ cup (60 g) crumbled cotija cheese
1 or 2 limes, cut into wedges for serving

Preheat the oven to 275°F (135°C). Season the brisket on all sides with salt and pepper. Heat the olive oil in a large ovenproof pot. Add the brisket to the pot and brown on both sides, about 5 minutes per side. Remove the brisket from the pot. Add the onion to the pot and cook, stirring occasionally, until browned, about 10 minutes. Add the garlic and cook for 2 minutes more. Add the vinegar and stir to deglaze the pan, scraping the bottom of the pan to incorporate all the pan drippings. Pour in the broth, tomatoes, and tomato paste and bring to a simmer. Add the cumin, paprika, coriander, cilantro, and bay leaf. Season with salt. Return the brisket to the pot (along with any accumulated juices), fat side up. Cover and transfer to the oven. Braise for 4 hours.

Remove the pot from the oven and carefully transfer the brisket to a large cutting board, reserving the liquid in the pot. Using two forks, shred the brisket in the direction of the grain (the meat should come apart easily). Return the shredded brisket to the pot and stir to incorporate with the juices. Return the pot to the oven and cook for 1 to 2 hours more, until very tender. Remove the pot from the oven and let rest for 10 minutes.

When ready to serve, in a small bowl, combine the sour cream, lime juice, and sea salt. Warm the tortillas in a skillet over medium heat for about 1 minute on each side.

Scoop some shredded brisket onto each tortilla. Garnish with the cabbage, a dollop of the sour cream mixture, pickled red onions, and a sprinkle of cotija cheese. Serve with wedges of lime on the side.

Shells

wood ear
oil-cured olive
pecorino

Serves 2

Market Variations
To make the market variations, replace the underlined ingredients with the items listed below. For more detail, see page 179.

Variation 1
maitake / niçoise olive / piave

Variation 2
morel / braised black olive / parmesan

These oversize shells are a bit of a nostalgic twist to an everyday pasta. Wood ear mushrooms, when they're available, are standouts. They have an elastic texture, literally resembling a floppy ear, and will sear well in a cast-iron skillet, resulting in a mushroom that is softened and a bit crispy as well. Any mushroom will work well here, but when spring's market presents morels, we highly recommend using those here, too. This dish can be served warm or at room temperature.

Sea salt
8 ounces (225 g) dried large pasta shells
2 tablespoons olive oil
1 pound (455 g) wood ear mushrooms, ends trimmed
1 cup (155 g) oil-cured olives
Cyprus flake salt
Extra-virgin olive oil
¼ cup (25 g) finely grated Pecorino cheese
¼ teaspoon black peppercorns, coarsely ground in a mortar and pestle
Black lava salt (optional)

Bring a large pot of salted water to a boil over high heat. Add the pasta and cook according to the package instructions.

Meanwhile, heat the olive oil in a large cast-iron skillet over high heat. Add the mushrooms and olives and season with flaky salt. Sauté until tender and crisp on the outside, 2 to 3 minutes. Remove from the heat.

Drain the pasta; season well with flaky salt and a good drizzle of olive oil. Add the pasta to the mushrooms and olives in the skillet and toss to combine.

Divide the shells and mushrooms between two plates and drizzle with extra-virgin olive oil. Top with the Pecorino and sprinkle with the peppercorns and black lava salt, if using.

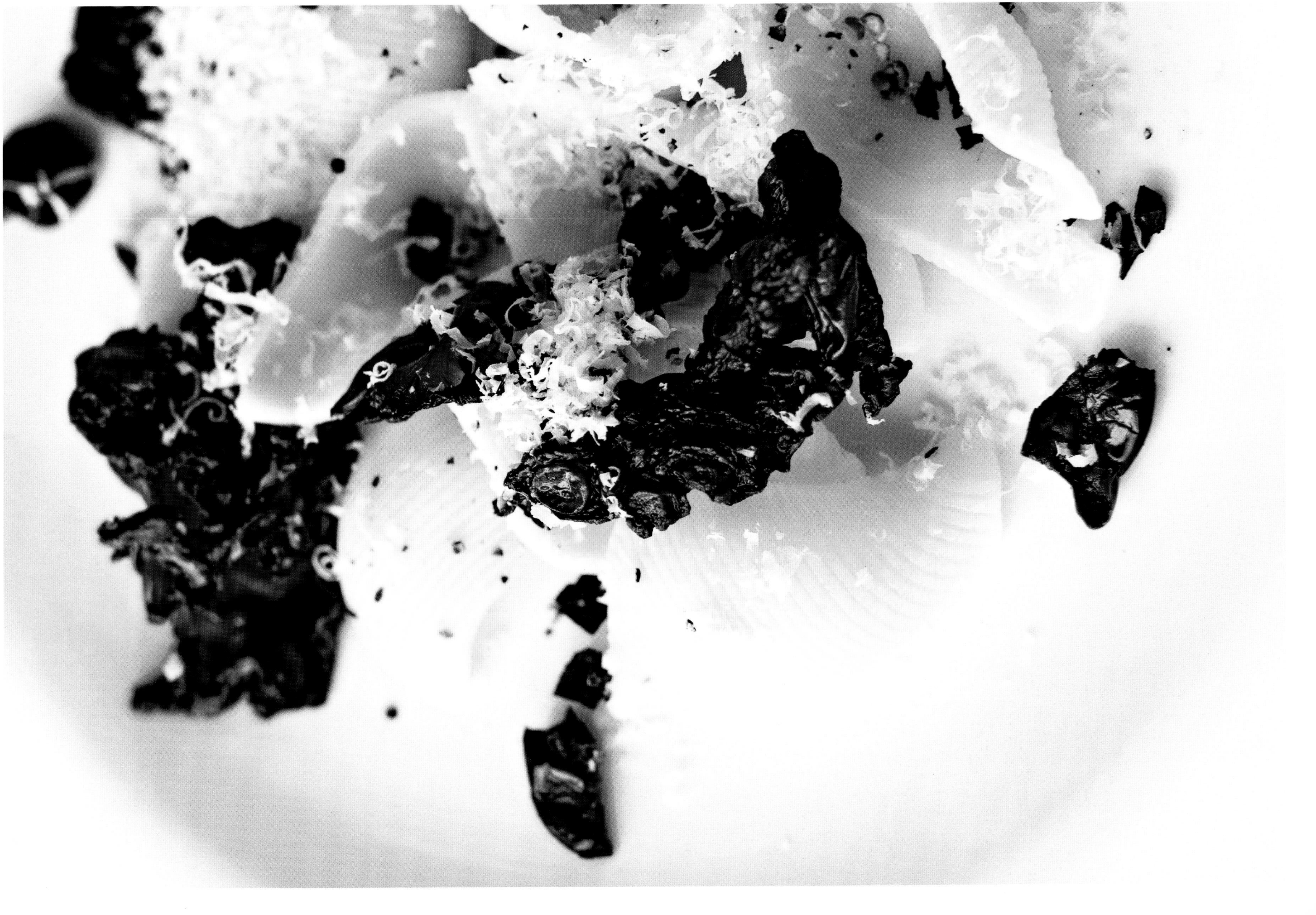

Lasagnette

san marzano
roasted garlic oil

Serves 2 to 4

Market Variations
To make the market variations, replace the underlined ingredients with the items listed below. For more detail, see page 179.

Variation 1
spaghetti / early girl tomato

Variation 2
pappardelle / roma tomato

The ingredients for this dish are usually stocked in our pantry for a quick weeknight meal, and the dish is also great for guests or a large group. If you keep a jar of the sauce in your refrigerator, this meal comes together in minutes. Make sure to use good-quality cans of Italian San Marzano tomatoes. When peak-of-summer tomatoes are abundant, we recommend making this dish using the season's best. If you have access to fresh lasagna noodles, use them (we pick up ours at Eataly in New York City, but small Italian grocers may offer them as well). This is a classic preparation, with a bit of depth added by the garlic oil; it is a slight but ever-memorable touch. Add a cheese plate and some crusty bread, and the meal is complete.

For the tomato sauce
2 (28-ounce / 785-g) cans San Marzano tomatoes
½ cup (120 ml) extra-virgin olive oil
2 tablespoons Cyprus flake salt
1 teaspoon sugar

Sea salt and olive oil, for cooking the noodles
1½ pounds (680 g) fresh lasagna noodles, sliced in half, or 1 pound (455 g) dry lasagnette noodles
2 tablespoons Garlic Confit oil (page 28)
1 cup (100 g) finely grated Parmesan cheese
1 teaspoon whole black peppercorns, coarsely ground in a mortar and pestle

For the sauce: In a large saucepan, combine the tomatoes, olive oil, and flaky salt and bring to a simmer over high heat. Reduce the heat to medium-low and cook, stirring occasionally, until the liquid from the tomatoes has reduced but the mixture is still a bit chunky, 20 to 30 minutes. Add the sugar and cook for 5 minutes more. Remove from the heat and use an immersion blender to blend the mixture to the desired consistency. (We like to keep ours a bit chunky.)

Meanwhile, bring a large pot of water to a boil over high heat and season well with sea salt and a good drizzle of olive oil. Add the lasagna noodles and cook until al dente, 2 to 3 minutes (or, if using dry noodles, according to the package instructions). Drain the noodles and transfer to a large bowl. Pour your desired amount of tomato sauce over the noodles and toss gently to combine.

Divide the noodles among two to four serving plates. Drizzle the garlic confit oil (generously) over each plate and garnish with the Parmesan and peppercorns.

Smoked Ricotta Gnudi

brown butter
<u>purple basil</u>

Serves 4

Market Variations
To make the market variations, replace the underlined ingredients with the items listed below. For more detail, see page 179.

Variation 1
tarragon

Variation 2
chive blossom

Variation 3
parsley

This recipe takes three days to prepare, so it requires a bit of planning. However, the process itself is quite simple—and is a truly memorable experience. The puffy pillows of ricotta will melt in your mouth, and the nuance of a smoked ricotta makes this a little different. This is a great meal to make for guests, as all the prep is done in advance. Salvatore Brooklyn makes a beautiful ricotta and a smoked variety as well. If you cannot find a smoked one, use all plain. And if you would like to make your own ricotta, see page 166.

3 cups (540 g) semolina flour
2 cups (455 g) ricotta, good-quality store-bought or homemade (page 166)
1 cup (245 g) good-quality smoked ricotta
Sea salt and freshly ground black pepper
1 cup (100 g) freshly grated Parmesan cheese
½ cup (1 stick / 115 g) unsalted butter, cut into tablespoons
Handful of fresh <u>purple basil</u>

Line a large or two smaller baking sheets with parchment paper. Spread 2 cups (360 g) of the semolina in an even layer over the parchment.

Combine the two ricottas in a large bowl. Line a plate (large enough to hold all the ricotta in a single layer) with a clean dish towel or a few layers of paper towel. Spread the ricotta over the towel and top with another clean dish towel or a thick layer of paper towels. Press down to remove any liquid from the ricotta. Return the ricotta to the bowl and season with salt and 3 or 4 grinds of pepper. Add the Parmesan and mix to incorporate.

Transfer the ricotta mixture to a piping bag fitted with a large round tip. Alternatively, transfer the mixture to a large zip-top bag (the bag should be large enough to leave half the bag empty when filled with the mixture). Push the ricotta down toward one corner of the bag and snip off the corner to make an opening. Pipe the ricotta over the semolina-lined baking sheet(s), snipping it with scissors as you pipe it to create logs that are about ½ inch (12 mm) long.

Sprinkle the remaining 1 cup (180 g) semolina evenly over the ricotta pieces. With your fingers, roll each piece into the semolina, rounding out the pieces, so that each side is completely covered with the semolina. Cover and refrigerate the gnudi for 3 days, until they are firm and dry.

When ready to serve, bring a large pot of water to a boil over high heat.

In a heavy-bottomed saucepan, melt the butter over medium-high heat. Stir continuously as the butter melts, then bubbles, and then begins to brown, 4 to 5 minutes. Turn off the heat and add the <u>basil</u>.

Salt the boiling water and add the gnudi, working in batches of four at a time. Cook until they rise to the top, about 4 minutes. Carefully remove the gnudi with a slotted spoon and add to the saucepan with the browned butter. Continue until all the gnudi are cooked. Divide the gnudi between serving plates and spoon the brown butter over top.

Aged Rib Eye

buffalo butter
pink and black peppercorn
lemon balm
watermelon radish

Serves 2

Market Variations
To make the market variations, replace the underlined ingredients with the items listed below. For more detail, see page 179.

Variation 1
green and black peppercorn / basil / black radish

Variation 2
wild peppercorn / parsley / purple radish

This method is a sure thing, and will create the char and crust of a grill, indoors. We do this on Friday nights or for a quick celebratory meal. Add some wild greens or arugula, and if you're feeling wildly indulgent, a great creamy burrata and a drizzle of saba will go very well.

1 teaspoon mixed whole pink and black peppercorns, coarsely crushed
   with a mortar and pestle
2 teaspoons coarse sea salt
1 bone-in rib eye steak
4 teaspoons olive oil
2 tablespoons salted butter
1 sprig fresh rosemary
2 sprigs fresh thyme
1 cup lemon balm leaves
1 watermelon radish, thinly shaved on a mandoline
2 cups (120 g) market greens
Cyprus flake salt

Place a large cast-iron skillet on the middle rack of the oven and preheat the oven to 500°F (260°C). Once the oven reaches temperature, carefully remove the hot skillet and set it on the stovetop over high heat for 5 minutes.

In a shallow bowl, combine the crushed peppercorns and sea salt.

Drizzle the steak on both sides with 2 teaspoons of the olive oil and then press both sides of the steak into the salt-and-pepper mixture to form a crust. Carefully place the steak in the hot skillet and sear for 1 minute on each side. Transfer the skillet to the oven and cook, undisturbed, for 2 minutes. Open the oven, flip the steak, and top with the butter, rosemary, and thyme. Cook until your desired doneness, about 2 minutes more for medium-rare, or until a thermometer inserted into the thickest part registers 135 to 140°F (57 to 60°C). Remove the steak from the skillet and cover loosely with aluminum foil. Let rest for 2 to 3 minutes.

In a small bowl, toss the lemon balm leaves and the shaved watermelon radish with the remaining 2 teaspoons of the olive oil.

Discard the herb sprigs and transfer the steak to a serving plate. Top with a pile of the greens, lemon balm, shaved radish, and a sprinkling of flaky salt.

Snacks

These are the nibbles we serve to guests or friends when they come over. When we are inviting friends and family to our home or studio, the focus should be on the company, so ease is integral here. Preparation is minimal, and the snacks are bright and fun. A well-executed cheese or meat platter and some other ideas are in the section ahead. You'll also find staples like Dukkah and Cured Eggs here (which we call upon in some recipes in the book) that are great to have on hand for easy canapés.

Cheese Board

A good cheese board needs little embellishment—the best are kept uncomplicated, highlighting beautiful ingredients in their simplest form. We recommend tasting and exploring at a local cheese purveyor. Here are some of our favorites. We opt to pull from a few categories to please a crowd—one creamy, one pungent, one salty, one firm, and one ashy, for some color and funk. If desired, feel free to add a seasonal fruit preserve, such as a fig compote, or a square of local honeycomb. We recommend arranging 4-ounce (115-g) wedges of each cheese on a large platter. Serve with your favorite crusty bread.

Ashville | De Glae Organic, Lancaster County
Semisoft sheep's-milk Camembert aged for between 2 months and 2 years; creamy and piquant, with an ash rind and buttery consistency.

Crème de Citeaux | Burgundy, France
Triple crème cow's-milk cheese; rich in butterfat, with subtle notes of white mushroom, this cheese is pillow soft and fresh in both flavor and look with its ivory, paper-thin rind.

Ouleout | Vulto Creamery
Named after the creek near the Delaware creamery from which it comes, Ouleout is a bold, oozy cheese made from raw, grass-fed cow's milk. Briny and stinky, this one is a favorite.

Tomme de Rabelais | France
Semisoft cow's-milk cheese; this is a milder, creamy white cheese, named in homage to the French satirist François Rabelais. The beautiful perforated rind offers a faintly bitter contrast to the cheese's fruity undertones.

Bleu Mont Cheddar | Bleu Mont Dairy Co., Wisconsin
"Bandaged" Cheddar aged for 16 months, giving it a sharpness that is rounded out with notes of caramel and moss from its beautiful rind.

Clockwise from top: Ashville, Crème de Cîteaux, Ouleout, Tomme de Rabelais, Bleu Mont Cheddar

Meat Board

Serves 4 to 6

Variety is key to a well-composed meat board—a spicy salami; a creamy, cured option like speck; and a bolder, more robust meat such as bresaola, to provide range. A briny olive paired with a sweet offering from the market, such as fresh figs, provides a bright balance to the deep flavors of the meat selection. Assemble a platter of 2 ounces (55 g) of each sliced variety and whole salami links with a sharp knife. Serve this with your favorite breads or crackers.

Fresh Black Mission Figs | These beautiful dark purple figs native to California are milder than the more abundant Brown Turkey varietal. Their peak season is from July to September.

Mortadella | A large Italian sausage from Bologna, made using a blend of heat-cured pork, lard, and a mélange of spices such as whole peppercorns and myrtle berries and, on occasion, pistachios.

Bresaola | An air-dried salted beef aged from 2 to 3 months. With a deep rust hue, this is a tender, lean meat with a gamier, robust flavor.

Speck | Produced in the South Tyrol region of northern Italy, speck is both dry-cured and smoked to provide its inimitable flavor. Softer and creamier than prosciutto, which is not smoked, it is the star of the region.

Hot Secchi Salami | Finely minced cured pork is combined with cracked chile and cayenne for a spicy but traditional take on salami.

Peppered Salami | Hand-rolled in cracked black peppercorns and laced with red wine, this is a classic and a favorite.

Clockwise from top: Fresh Black Mission Figs, Mortadella, Bresaola, Speck, Hot Secchi Salami, Peppered Salami

Charred Eggplant Puree

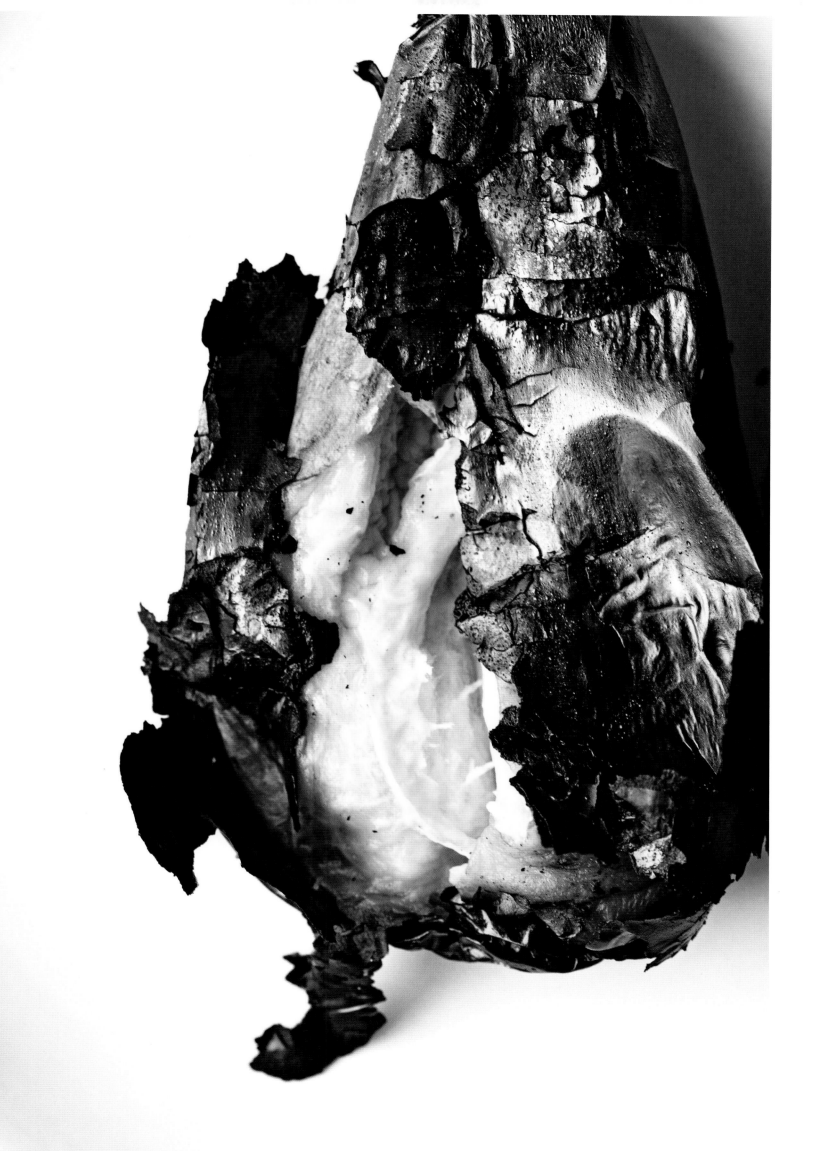

Charred Eggplant Puree

Serves 2 to 4

This eggplant dish, also known at Middle Eastern tables as baba ghanoush, is simple and rustic. The aroma of charring in this manner will fill your home and impart a truly incredible flavor to the dish. We serve this with warm bread and herbs as a starter, or as a puree under main dishes like poultry, fish, and octopus. Be sure to use a good pair of kitchen tongs for this project.

3 globe eggplants, 1 to 1½ pounds (450 to 680 g) each
Juice of ½ lemon
1 tablespoon tahini
1 tablespoon olive oil
Sea salt and freshly ground black pepper

Use a fork to prick the eggplants all over. Turn a stovetop burner to medium-high and, using tongs, place the eggplants directly over the burner, using the tongs to rotate them frequently, until charred, 7 to 10 minutes for each. Allow the eggplants to cool slightly, then halve them lengthwise and use a fork to scoop the flesh into a large bowl. Add the lemon juice, tahini, and olive oil and whisk with the fork until incorporated and smooth. Season with salt and pepper.

Braised Black Olives

Serves 2 to 4

This is a favorite in our kitchen; braising the olives softens them and brings out a depth of flavor, which is further enhanced with herbs and lemon. This can be served with cheese and bread for guests, or be incorporated into main dishes like our Octopus (page 92) and Niçoise Salad (page 97).

3 tablespoons olive oil
1 cup (155 g) Niçoise olives
Pinch of red pepper flakes
3 sprigs fresh thyme
2 sprigs fresh rosemary
1 lemon
¼ cup (60 ml) dry white wine

Heat the olive oil in a medium saucepan over medium-high heat. Add the olives, pepper flakes, thyme, and rosemary. Peel ribbons of zest from the lemon, avoiding the bitter white pith, and add them to the pan. Squeeze the juice from half the lemon and strain it into the saucepan. Cook for 1 minute, until fragrant, then add the wine. Reduce the heat to low, cover, and cook for about 20 minutes, until the olives are soft. Serve immediately.

Burrata

fried basil
lemon oil

Serves 4 to 6

The word *burrata* means "buttered" in Italian, which perfectly describes the creaminess of this cheese. We love it in its utmost simplicity, enhanced only slightly by a bit of basil and lemon oil. Serve this with a wonderful bread and enjoy immediately.

¾ cup (180 ml) olive oil
Peels from 2 lemons
8 to 10 fresh basil leaves
2 (8-ounce / 225-g) balls burrata
Cyprus flake salt
Warm, crusty bread, for serving

In a small saucepan, combine ½ cup (120 ml) of the olive oil and the lemon peels. Warm over low heat for 10 to 15 minutes, until the oil is infused and fragrant. Remove from the heat and let cool.

In a small sauté pan, heat the remaining ¼ cup (60 ml) of the olive oil over medium-high heat. Once it starts to shimmer, add the basil and fry until crisp, about 30 seconds. Remove using a slotted spoon and drain on paper towels.

To serve, arrange the burrata on a serving platter and tear them open. Drizzle with some of the lemon oil and top with fried basil leaves and a sprinkling of flaky salt. Serve with warm, crusty bread.

Cured Eggs

black peppercorn
bay leaf

Makes 12 eggs

Market Variations
To make the market variations, replace the underlined ingredients with the items listed below. For more detail, see page 180.

Variation 1 – pink
beet

Variation 2 – yellow
saffron

These colorful eggs add a bit of punch and tartness to any meal. We love them in salads, on decadent toasts, and in our soups. To serve as a canapé, cut them in half, dollop with some crème fraîche, and sprinkle with good sea salt.

12 large eggs, hard boiled (page 26)
1 cup (240 ml) distilled white vinegar
1 teaspoon sugar
½ teaspoon sea salt
½ teaspoon black peppercorns
1 bay leaf
Cyprus flake salt, for serving

When the eggs are cool, peel them and place them in a large jar.

In a 2 quart (2 L) saucepan, combine the vinegar, sugar, salt, peppercorns, bay leaf, and 3 quarts (2.8 L) water and bring to a boil. Reduce the heat to medium; cover and simmer for 20 minutes. Uncover and let cool completely.

Pour the mixture into the jar, covering the eggs completely, and refrigerate for at least 2 hours, stirring gently once or twice for even pickling.

To serve, slice the eggs in half and top with flaky salt.

Storage – *Refrigerate in a sealed container for up to 1 month.*

Cured Eggs – Top: Variation 1, Bottom: Variation 2

Dukkah

<u>white sesame</u>
<u>coconut flake</u>
<u>pine nut</u>
<u>almond</u>
<u>chamomile</u>
sea salt

Makes about 1 cup (115 g)

Market Variations
To make the market variations, replace the underlined ingredients with the items listed below. For more detail, see page 180.

Variation 1 – black
black sesame seed / poppy seed / pine nut / almond / walnut

Variation 2 – green
pistachio / hemp seed / sesame seed / rose petal / cinnamon

Variation 3 – earth
hazelnut / walnut / coriander / white sesame seed

Dukkah is a favorite staple in our kitchens. It is rooted in Mediterranean food and usually includes a variety of spices and nuts. Ours is a bit different from the traditional combination, with a few playful additions. Inspired by color and flavor, we keep jars of it around for quick sprinkles. Use this on toast, over eggs, in salads, on yogurt (as shown), or on pretty much anything.

½ cup (75 g) <u>white sesame seeds</u>
¼ cup (20 g) <u>unsweetened coconut flakes</u>, crushed with a mortar and pestle
1 tablespoon <u>pine nuts</u>, lightly toasted and finely chopped
1 tablespoon <u>slivered almonds</u>, finely chopped
2 teaspoons dried <u>chamomile</u>, whole or crushed
¼ teaspoon sea salt

In a small bowl, combine all the ingredients until thoroughly mixed.

Storage – *Store in a sealed container at room temperature for 3 to 6 months.*

Desserts

To end a meal on a sweet note, we've collected a few of our very favorite desserts. Some are warm bowls, like the Sahleb, and others are bright and refreshing, like the carrot and beetroot ice creams. Our sweets are inspired by fruit, vegetable, and color. We love the play of textures, layered upon each other—and almost always a sprinkle of salt atop any sweet to add balance. These plates are light and fragrant, perfect for the season.

Sahleb

<u>rose water</u>
<u>coconut</u>
<u>pistachio</u>
<u>ceylon cinnamon</u>

Serves 4 to 6

Market Variations
To make the market variations, replace the underlined ingredients with the items listed below. For more detail, see page 180.

Variation 1
orange blossom water / hemp seed / white sesame seed / nutmeg

Variation 2
agave nectar / dukkah / black sesame seed / muscovado sugar

Variation 3
honey / dried fig / almond / ginger

This warm, pudding-like dessert brings me back to summer nights in Jerusalem. At local spots and late-night eateries, it is often served in paper cups to patrons who sit roadside on small stools. It is the perfect sweet ending on a chilly summer night. If you would like to replace the sugar with honey or maple syrup, simply use 1 tablespoon of either. Mahlab, an aromatic spice made from the seeds of sour wild cherries, is sold at local boutique spice shops or Middle Eastern grocers. If you can find it, it adds a floral essence to the dish; otherwise it can be omitted or replaced with ground cardamom.

1½ tablespoons cornstarch
2 cups (480 ml) unsweetened, full-fat coconut milk
1 tablespoon sugar
½ teaspoon mahlab powder (optional)
1 teaspoon <u>rose water</u>
2 tablespoons <u>pistachios</u>, chopped
2 tablespoons <u>flaked unsweetened coconut</u>
Ground <u>Ceylon cinnamon</u>
Peruvian pink salt

In a small bowl, whisk the cornstarch into ½ cup (120 ml) of the coconut milk. Pour the remaining 1½ cups (360 ml) coconut milk into a small saucepan and add the sugar. Bring to a boil over medium-high heat. Stir the cornstarch mixture to loosen up any starch that has settled on the bottom and add it to the pan. Stir in the mahlab, if using, and reduce the heat to medium. Cook, whisking continuously to keep lumps from forming, for 10 to 15 minutes, until the mixture thickens. Add the <u>rose water</u> and stir to incorporate.

Serve in individual cups or small bowls. Scatter the <u>pistachios</u>, <u>coconut</u>, <u>cinnamon</u>, and pink salt over the top and serve warm.

Burnt Apricot

whipped yogurt
puffed amaranth
maple
salt

Serves 6

Market Variations
To make the market variations, replace the underlined ingredients with the items listed below. For more detail, see page 180.

Variation 1
nectarine / toasted buckwheat

Variation 2
peach / puffed millet

Variation 3
fig / dukkah

Charred fruit is perfect for summer. It is a light dessert and great for a crowd. The whipped yogurt is reason enough to make this meal. It could even be viewed as a truly decadent breakfast.

1 cup (240 ml) plain Greek yogurt
½ cup (120 ml) heavy cream
6 apricots, halved and pitted
6 tablespoons (¾ stick / 85 g) unsalted butter, melted
1 tablespoon olive oil
1½ teaspoons brown sugar
6 tablespoons (90 ml) maple syrup
¼ cup (4 g) puffed amaranth
Cyprus flake salt

In a large bowl, beat together the yogurt and cream with a hand mixer or a whisk until the mixture increases in volume and forms soft peaks. Set aside.

Heat a cast-iron skillet over medium-high heat. In a medium bowl, toss the apricot halves with the butter, olive oil, and sugar until completely coated. Place the apricots cut side down in the hot skillet and cook, turning once, until the fruit has softened and the outside is lightly charred, 5 to 7 minutes per side. Remove the apricots from the skillet.

Alternatively, the apricots can be prepared under the broiler. Place the halves cut side up on a baking sheet and broil on high until the fruit has softened and the top is caramelized, about 15 minutes.

To serve, dollop a spoonful of the whipped yogurt onto each of six serving plates. Arrange two apricot halves over the yogurt. Finish with a drizzle of maple syrup and a sprinkling of puffed amaranth and flaky salt. Alternatively, you can serve this dessert communally on a large platter.

Banana Bread

dark chocolate
crème fraîche
cyprus salt

Makes 1 loaf

Market Variations
To make the market variations, replace the underlined ingredients with the items listed below. For more detail, see page 180.

Variation 1
walnut / yogurt / black salt

Variation 2
almond / mascarpone / pink salt

Banana bread is a comforting classic, perfect to make on a Sunday at home and the best gift for a neighbor or friend. This one is a favorite and comes together in minutes, no stand mixer needed. The crusty top is the star here. Also, be sure to use overripe bananas and mash them quite well—doing this releases the moisture from the bananas to create a moist bread. One way to always have ripe bananas on hand is to freeze peeled, overripe bananas in a zip-top bag; once they're defrosted, be sure to use any liquid you find in the bag as well.

½ cup (1 stick / 115 g) salted butter, at room temperature, plus more for greasing
4 overripe bananas, mashed, or 4 frozen bananas, defrosted, with their liquid
¾ cup (165 g) packed dark brown sugar
2 eggs
1 teaspoon pure vanilla extract
¼ teaspoon fine sea salt
1 teaspoon baking soda
1½ cups (190 g) all-purpose flour
1 cup (240 ml) plain yogurt, good-quality store-bought or homemade (page 164)
3 ounces (85 g) semisweet dark chocolate, chopped into chunks
¼ teaspoon ground cinnamon
2 tablespoons superfine sugar

For serving
8 ounces (225 g) crème fraîche, good-quality store-bought or homemade (page 164)
Cyprus flake salt

Preheat the oven to 350°F (175°C). Grease a 4 x 8-inch (10 x 20-cm) loaf pan with butter.

In a large bowl using a wooden spoon, stir together the bananas and butter until well combined.

Add the sugar, eggs, vanilla, and sea salt. Sprinkle the baking soda over the mixture, followed by the flour, and stir well. Fold in the yogurt and chocolate.

In a small bowl, mix the cinnamon and superfine sugar together.

Pour the batter into the prepared pan and sprinkle the cinnamon-sugar mixture over the top. Bake until golden brown, 55 to 65 minutes, or until a toothpick inserted into the center comes out clean. Let cool in the pan for 20 minutes.

Remove the bread from the pan; slice and serve each piece garnished with 1 tablespoon of the crème fraîche and flaky salt.

Storage – *Best enjoyed immediately. If storage is necessary, keep in a sealed container refrigerated for up to 5 days and reheat to serve.*

Dark Chocolate Olive Oil Cake

<u>pistachio</u>
<u>rose</u>
<u>cardamom cream</u>
cyprus salt

Serves 8

Market Variations
To make the market variations, replace the underlined ingredients with the items listed below. For more detail, see page 180.

Variation 1
macadamia / violet / crème fraîche

Variation 2
hazelnut / hibiscus / mascarpone

This beautiful and simple chocolate cake embodies a balance of sweet and savory. We love using a rich extra-virgin olive oil and a great-quality chocolate for the utmost flavor. Top this cake with any wild or seasonal fruit, petals, and crème of your choice to make it perfect for a party or festive celebration.

¾ cup (180 ml) extra-virgin olive oil, plus more for greasing the pan
½ cup (70 g) good-quality unsweetened cocoa powder
½ cup (120 ml) boiling water
1 tablespoon pure vanilla extract
⅓ cups (165 g) all-purpose flour
½ teaspoon baking soda
1 teaspoon sea salt
1 cup (195 g) superfine sugar
3 large eggs
Cyprus flake salt

For the <u>cardamom cream</u>
½ cup (120 ml) heavy cream
½ teaspoon ground cardamom

For serving
1 teaspoon <u>dried rose petals</u>
½ cup (65 g) chopped unsalted <u>pistachios</u>
Cyprus flake salt

Preheat the oven to 325°F (165°C). Grease a 9-inch (23-cm) springform baking pan with a little olive oil and line the base with parchment paper cut to fit.

Sift the cocoa into a medium bowl and whisk in the boiling water until smooth. Whisk in the vanilla, then set aside to cool slightly. In a separate large bowl, combine the flour, baking soda, and salt.

In the bowl of a stand mixer fitted with the paddle attachment, beat together the sugar, olive oil, and eggs until you have a light, fluffy cream, about 3 minutes.

Turn the speed on the mixer down and pour in the cocoa and vanilla mixture. Slowly add the flour mixture until it is evenly incorporated, stopping the mixer and scraping down the bowl as necessary.

Pour the batter into the prepared pan and sprinkle with flaky salt. Bake for 30 to 35 minutes, or until the sides are set and the top of the cake still looks slightly moist. A cake tester inserted into the center should come out clean or with just a few crumbs on it. Let cool in the pan on a wire rack for 10 minutes.

While the cake is baking, in a chilled metal or glass bowl using a hand mixer, beat the cream on medium speed until soft peaks form, about 4 minutes. Add the cardamom and beat until stiff peaks form, about 1 to 2 minutes more. Cover and refrigerate until ready to serve.

Run a knife around the edge of the cake and release the sides of the pan. Transfer the cake to a serving plate or cake stand. Sprinkle with more flaky salt. Serve each slice with a dollop of the <u>cardamom cream</u> and a sprinkling of <u>rose petals</u>, <u>pistachios</u>, and flaky salt.

Roasted Ice Cream, two ways with seeds

no. 1
carrot
hazelnut
sesame seed crumble

no. 2
beet
pistachio
sunflower seed crumble

Makes 1 quart (960 ml)

These colorful ice creams bring forth an unexpected flavor profile to traditional ice cream. Be assured, the classic sweetness and creaminess are still apparent, but here they are combined with a subtle earthiness and unexpected charm. Served with a crunchy-sweet seed crumble, each bite is divine.

no. 1 | Roasted Carrot Ice Cream

For the carrot ice cream
12 carrots (about 1 pound / 455 g)
2 tablespoons olive oil
4 tablespoons honey
4 egg yolks
4 cups (960 ml) heavy cream
¾ cup (150 g) granulated sugar
1 vanilla bean, seeds scraped and pod reserved

For the hazelnut sesame seed crumble
½ cup (100 g) granulated sugar
½ cup (110 g) packed light brown sugar
2 tablespoons unsalted butter
½ cup (55 g) unsalted chopped hazelnuts
1 cup (150 g) white sesame seeds

Peruvian pink salt, to garnish

For the ice cream: Preheat the oven to 400°F (205°C). Line a baking sheet with parchment paper.

Toss the carrots with the olive oil and 1 tablespoon of the honey and arrange them in a single layer on the prepared baking sheet. Roast, turning once halfway through, until tender and just starting to caramelize, about 35 minutes. Remove from the oven and let cool. Transfer the carrots to a food processor and process into a smooth puree. Measure 1 cup (240 ml) of the puree and set aside.

In a medium bowl, whisk the egg yolks until smooth. Set aside.

In a 3-quart (2.8-L) saucepan, combine 3 cups (720 ml) of the cream, the sugar, vanilla bean pod and seeds, and the remaining 3 tablespoons of honey. Whisk in the reserved 1 cup (240 ml) of carrot puree until completely incorporated. Attach a candy thermometer to the pot and heat the mixture over medium-low heat, stirring frequently, until it reaches about 130°F (55°C). Remove the pan from the heat and, while whisking, slowly drizzle about one-quarter of the cream mixture into the egg yolks. Pour the egg yolks and cream back into the pan and stir with a wooden spoon to combine. Return to the heat and continue to cook, stirring continuously, until the mixture reaches between 170°F (75°C) and 175°F (80°C). Do not go above this range or the egg yolks may scramble. Immediately remove from the heat and stir in the remaining 1 cup (240 ml) cream. Strain the mixture through a fine-mesh sieve into a glass container, cover, and refrigerate overnight.

Churn the chilled ice cream base in an ice cream maker according to the manufacturer's instructions. Scrape the ice cream into a jar or pan, cover with a piece of plastic wrap or parchment paper pressed directly to the surface of the ice cream, and freeze until firm, about 3 hours.

For the crumble: Preheat the oven to 350°F (180°C). Line a baking sheet with parchment paper.

In a small saucepan, combine both sugars, the butter, and ½ cup (120 ml) water. Bring to a boil over medium heat, stirring continuously, until the sugars have completely dissolved. Stir in the nuts and sesame seeds, remove from the heat, and pour onto the prepared baking sheet. Use a spatula to spread the nuts and seeds into an even layer. Bake for 10 to 12 minutes, until the syrup has set and is lightly golden. Remove from the oven and let cool. Once cool, break the brittle into pieces and transfer to a food processor. Process until finely ground.

To serve, scoop the ice cream into bowls and top with a sprinkling of the crumble and pink salt.

no. 2 | Roasted Beetroot Ice Cream

For the beet ice cream
3 medium beets, about 1 pound (455 g) total
4 egg yolks
4 cups (960 ml) heavy cream
½ cup (100 g) granulated sugar
2 tablespoons honey
1 vanilla bean, seeds scraped and pod reserved

For the pistachio sunflower seed crumble
½ cup (100 g) granulated sugar
½ cup (110 g) packed light brown sugar
2 tablespoons unsalted butter
½ cup (65 g) unsalted raw pistachios
1 cup (140 g) hulled unsalted sunflower seeds

Peruvian pink salt, to garnish

For the ice cream: Preheat the oven to 400°F (205°C).

Wash and dry the beets and cut off and discard their greens. Set them in a deep baking dish or pie plate in a single layer. Add enough water so that the beets are half covered, but not fully submerged. Cover the baking dish tightly with aluminum foil and place in the oven. Roast the beets for 1 hour, or until fork-tender. Remove them from the oven and let cool. Peel the beets with a paring knife or by rubbing the skin off with a paper towel. Quarter the beets and transfer them to a food processor. Process into a smooth puree. Measure 1¼ cups (300 ml) of the puree and set aside.

In a medium bowl, whisk the egg yolks until smooth. Set aside.

In a 3-quart (2.8-L) saucepan, combine 3 cups (720 ml) of the cream, the sugar, honey, and vanilla bean pod and seeds. Whisk in the reserved 1¼ cups (300 ml) of beet puree until completely incorporated. Attach a candy thermometer to the pot and heat the mixture over medium-low heat, stirring frequently, until it reaches about 130°F (55°C). Remove the pan from the heat and, while whisking, slowly drizzle about one-quarter of the cream mixture into the egg yolks. Pour the egg yolks and cream back into the pan and stir with a wooden spoon to combine. Return to the heat and continue to cook, stirring continuously, until the mixture reaches between 170°F (75°C) and 175°F (80°C). Do not go above this range or the egg yolks may scramble. Immediately remove from the heat and stir in the remaining 1 cup (240 ml) cream. Strain the mixture through a fine-mesh sieve into a glass container, cover, and refrigerate overnight.

Churn the chilled ice cream base in an ice cream maker according to the manufacturer's instructions. Scrape the ice cream into a jar or pan, cover with a piece of plastic wrap or parchment paper pressed directly to the surface of the ice cream, and freeze until firm, about 3 hours.

For the crumble: Preheat the oven to 350°F (180°C). Line a baking sheet with parchment paper.

In a small saucepan, combine both sugars, the butter, and ½ cup (120 ml) water. Bring to a boil over medium heat, stirring continuously, until the sugars have completely dissolved. Stir in the nuts and sunflower seeds, remove from the heat, and pour onto the prepared baking sheet. Use a spatula to spread the nuts and seeds into an even layer. Bake for 10 to 12 minutes, until the syrup has set and is lightly golden. Remove from the oven and let cool. Once cool, break the brittle into pieces and transfer to a food processor. Process until finely ground.

To serve, scoop the ice cream into bowls and top with a sprinkling of the crumble and pink salt.

Storage – *Both ice creams will keep for 1 to 2 months in the freezer and the crumbles will keep for up to 2 weeks in a sealed container.*

Dairy

Making your own dairy products is truly not as daunting as it sounds. Besides providing a sense of accomplishment, it allows us to be in control of the ingredients and kind of milk that go into our dairy products. The homemade varieties of yogurts and cheeses are creamier and richer than any you find in a shop. Most of these will keep for quite a while in the refrigerator. They also make great neighborly gifts.

Crème Fraîche

Makes 2 cups (480 ml)

We use this creamy goodness almost every day in both a sweet and savory capacity. Use it on toast, in salads and soups, and as a dollop on your dessert. The homemade variety is incredibly easy to make and offers a richer tanginess than the store-bought kind.

2 cups (480 ml) heavy cream (pasteurized, not ultra-pasteurized, if possible)
2 tablespoons cultured buttermilk or cultured full-fat plain yogurt

In a medium bowl, mix together the cream and buttermilk. Pour the mixture into a glass jar or plastic container. Place in a warm room, partially covered, and let sit for 12 to 24 hours, until thickened and slightly tangy.

Storage – *Refrigerate in a sealed container for 7 to 10 days.*

Yogurt

Makes about 2 quarts (2 L)

Homemade yogurt can be made overnight with very few ingredients. Be sure to start with a yogurt that contains live cultures for maximum health benefits.

2 quarts (2 L) whole milk
½ cup (120 ml) full-fat plain yogurt containing active cultures

In a Dutch oven with a candy thermometer clipped to the side, warm the milk over medium heat, stirring, until it just starts to bubble around the edges, about 200°F (90°C). Remove from the heat and let cool to about 115°F (45°C), stirring occasionally to prevent a skin from forming.

Transfer 1 cup (240 ml) of the milk to a small bowl. Add the yogurt and whisk until smooth. Pour the yogurt mixture back into the Dutch oven and whisk gently to combine with the warm milk.

Cover the Dutch oven with a lid and wrap in a large dish towel. (This will insulate the milk and keep it warm.) Ideally, the milk should stay around 110°F (43°C). Place the pot in the oven with the heat off and let rest, undisturbed, for 4 to 12 hours to set. It will get thicker and tangier as it sits. After 4 hours, check the yogurt. If you find it to be too loose, replace the lid, rewrap with the towel, and return to the oven to continue to set. Continue checking the yogurt every hour until it has reached your desired tanginess and consistency. Drain the whey from the top or whisk it back into the yogurt until smooth. Transfer the yogurt to a large container, cover, and refrigerate.

Storage – *Refrigerate in a sealed container for up to 2 weeks.*

Ricotta

Makes 1 cup (245 g)

Ricotta is called for in many of our recipes. It is the base for our pancakes, and we spread it on many toasts. If you are able to find a high-quality handmade variety at your local store, that is the second-best option. However, should you take on the endeavor, making your own at home is quite simple and delicious.

1 quart (960 ml) whole milk
1 cup (240 ml) heavy cream
½ teaspoon fine sea salt
½ teaspoon sugar
3 tablespoons distilled white vinegar

Line a large sieve with a layer of fine-mesh cheesecloth and set it over a large bowl.

In a heavy 6-quart (5.7-L) pot, combine the milk, cream, salt, and sugar and bring to a boil over medium heat, stirring occasionally to prevent scorching. Add the vinegar and reduce the heat to low. Simmer, stirring continuously, until the mixture curdles, 2 to 4 minutes.

Pour the mixture into the lined sieve and let drain for 1 hour.

Discard the liquid in the bowl or keep the whey for another use. Transfer the ricotta to a jar, cover, and refrigerate.

Storage – *Refrigerate in a sealed container for up to 5 days.*

Marinated Labneh

Makes 14 or 15 (1-ounce/28-g) balls

This marinated yogurt is a constant in our refrigerator. Labneh is a Lebanese form of strained yogurt, and here we preserve it in olive oil and herbs. The tangy, creamy yogurt can be spread on toast or served under roasted vegetables and in a salad. It can also be served with warm pita along with other mezze. Traditionally, it is often included in Middle Eastern breakfasts. It also pairs well with spices like red pepper flakes, sumac, and za'atar.

1 32-ounce (900-g) container full-fat plain Greek yogurt
2 teaspoons sea salt
2 bay leaves
2 sprigs rosemary
2 sprigs oregano
2 garlic cloves, peeled
2 cups (480 ml) extra-virgin olive oil

In a medium bowl, stir together the yogurt and salt. Lay out two layers of cheesecloth on a work surface and spoon the yogurt into the middle. Gather up the edges of the cheesecloth to enclose the yogurt and tie with a string. Tie the string to a wooden spoon and rest the spoon on top of a large bowl, so that the ball is suspended over the bowl. Place in the refrigerator to drain for 3 days.

Unwrap the ball and discard the cheesecloth. Roll the yogurt into 2-tablespoon balls, about the size of golf balls, and place them on a parchment paper-lined baking sheet. Refrigerate for 3 hours, uncovered, to dry.

Remove the balls from the refrigerator and transfer to a large glass jar. Add the herbs and garlic, and cover with the olive oil. Seal the jar and marinate the labneh in the refrigerator for 24 hours before using.

Storage – *Refrigerate the labneh in its marinating oil for up to 3 weeks.*

Cook's Notes

In this section, you can find information such as amounts and helpful tips on how to prepare the market variations listed in the recipes throughout the book. The original ingredients are the underlined items in the recipe text, which can be replaced by the variation ingredients. The variation ingredients can be prepared or used in the dish in the same manner as the original recipe, unless otherwise specified, and are listed in the same order as the ingredients they are intended to replace.

Cook's Notes – Breakfast

Poached Eggs

The millet and amaranth can be purchased puffed and do not require toasting. To make the variations, pour the yogurt or crème fraîche into a shallow bowl, top with the eggs, and garnish, using the alternative options below in place of the original ingredients.

Original ingredients
black quinoa
toasted buckwheat
kefir
fermented kraut
pepita

Variation 1
½ cup (100 g) cooked white quinoa (page 25)
¼ cup (4 g) puffed amaranth
¼ cup (60 ml) plain yogurt
2 tablespoons Pickled Red Onion (page 32)
1 tablespoon black sesame seeds

Variation 2
½ cup (100 g) cooked farro (page 25)
¼ cup (4 g) puffed millet
¼ cup (60 ml) crème fraîche, good-quality store-bought or homemade (page 164)
¼ avocado, sliced
2 tablespoons hazelnuts, toasted and chopped

Fruit Salad

For the variations, assemble the ingredients in the same manner as the original and drizzle the ricotta with honey.

Original ingredients
cantaloupe
rainier cherry
golden raspberry

Variation 1
1 plum, cut into wedges
2 figs, halved or quartered
¼ cup (35 g) pine berries

Variation 2
1 wedge honeydew melon
½ cup (70 g) boysenberries
¼ cup (35 g) gooseberries

Variation 3
1 wedge watermelon
½ cup (70 g) strawberries
½ apple, sliced

Green Shakshuka

To make the variations, the original ingredients can be replaced by the alternative options below.

Original ingredients
wild greens
leek

Variation 1
½ medium head green cabbage, shredded
3 spring onions, chopped

Variation 2
12 ounces (340 g) young spinach
1 bunch ramps, chopped

Variation 3
12 ounces (340 g) dandelion greens
½ red onion, chopped

Breakfast Board

To make the variations, the original ingredients can be replaced by the alternative options below.

Original ingredients
salmon
trout
whitefish roe

Variation 1
¼ pound (115 g) smoked sable
¼ pound (115 g) smoked whitefish
1 ounce (28 g) salmon roe

Variation 2
¼ pound (115 g) gravlax
¼ pound (115 g) peppered mackerel
1 ounce (28 g) trout roe

Buttered Eggs

To make the variations, the original ingredients can be replaced by the alternative options below.

Original ingredients
rye
pecorino

Variation 1
2 slices sourdough bread
Grated Manchego cheese

Variation 2
2 slices buckwheat bread
Grated Parmesan cheese

Soft-Boiled Eggs

To make the variations, the original ingredients can be replaced by the alternative options below.

Original ingredients
labneh
breakfast radish
pine nut

Variation 1
1 tablespoon Mascarpone cheese
½ cup (60 g) black radishes, sliced
2 teaspoons hazelnuts, toasted and halved

Variation 2
1 tablespoon crème fraîche, good-quality store-bought or homemade (page 164)
½ cup (60 g) purple radishes, sliced
2 teaspoons slivered almonds

Variation 3
1 tablespoon yogurt, good-quality store-bought or homemade (page 164)
½ cup (60 g) red radishes, sliced
2 teaspoons Dukkah (page 146)

Slow-Cooked Oat Porridge

To make the variations, prepare the oats as directed, then top with maple syrup, honeycomb, and butter. The original toppings can be replaced by the alternative options below.

Original ingredients
white sesame
chamomile
cyprus salt

Variation 1
1 tablespoon black sesame seeds
2 tablespoons dried currants
¼ teaspoon black lava salt

Variation 2
2 tablespoons pistachios, chopped
1 teaspoon rose petals (fresh or dry)
¼ teaspoon pink salt

Smoothie Bowl

To make the variations, the original ingredients can be replaced by the alternative options below. Not all variations will have the same number of ingredients, but all can be prepared in the same way and finished with their corresponding topping.

Original ingredients
espresso
maca
cinnamon
maple
banana
almond milk

topping
hazelnut
cocoa nib

Variation 1 – white
2 tablespoons Greek yogurt
2 dates, pitted
1 banana, frozen
Seeds from 1 vanilla bean
1 teaspoon ground cardamom
½ cup (120 ml) unsweetened cashew milk

topping
1 tablespoon puffed millet
1 tablespoon hemp seeds

Variation 2 – tea
1 tablespoon rooibos tea leaves
1 banana, frozen
3 dates, pitted
½ cup (120 ml) unsweetened coconut milk
1 tablespoon honey

topping
1 tablespoon puffed amaranth
1 tablespoon rooibos tea leaves

Variation 3 – fruit
½ cup (120 ml) kefir
1 cup (155 g) pitted sweet cherries, frozen
Seeds from 1 vanilla bean
3 dried figs, chopped

topping
1 tablespoon black sesame seeds
1 tablespoon pitted sweet cherries, frozen
1 tablespoon honey

Toast and Roasted Fruit Jam

To make the variations, the original ingredients can be replaced by the alternative options below.

Original ingredients
blueberry
balsamic
basil

Variation 1
4 cups (560 g) fresh blackberries
2 teaspoons red wine vinegar
2 sprigs tarragon

Variation 2
4 cups (560 g) fresh red gooseberries
2 teaspoons white wine vinegar
2 sprigs thyme

Wilted Flower Yogurt Bowl

To make the variations, the original ingredients can be replaced by the alternative options below.

Original ingredients
petals
pistachio
black sesame
maple

Variation 1
1 teaspoon chamomile flowers (fresh or dried)
1 tablespoon almonds, chopped
1 teaspoon white sesame seeds
1 teaspoon honey

Variation 2
1 teaspoon rose petals (fresh or dried)
1 tablespoon macadamia nuts, chopped
1 teaspoon poppy seeds
1 teaspoon agave nectar

Variation 3
1 teaspoon apple blossoms (fresh or dried)
1 tablespoon walnuts, chopped
½ teaspoon bee pollen
1 teaspoon date syrup

Buckwheat Bread

To make the variations, the original ingredients can be replaced by the alternative options below. The chamomile and cornflowers can be mixed into the honey in the same fashion as the rose petals.

Original ingredients
buckwheat bread
rose honey

Variation 1
1 slice sprouted sourdough
¼ cup (10 g) fresh chamomile flowers, or 2 tablespoons dried

Variation 2
1 slice walnut loaf
¼ cup (10 g) fresh cornflowers, or 2 tablespoons dried

Ricotta Pancakes

For the variations, the rhubarb and grapes can be prepared in the same method as the blackberries in the original recipe, switching the thyme for the alternative herbs listed below. Garnish the pancakes with the crème fraîche and the topping variations given below.

Original ingredients
blackberry
thyme
hazelnut

Variation 1
1 cup (110 g) diced rhubarb stems
2 sprigs fresh mint, plus more for garnish, leaves chopped or torn
¼ cup (30 g) walnuts, toasted and chopped

Variation 2
1 cup (150 g) grapes
2 sprigs fresh basil, plus more for garnish, leaves chopped or torn
¼ cup (30 g) almonds, toasted and chopped

Cook's Notes – Toasts

Avocado Toast

To make the variations, the original ingredients can be replaced by the alternative options below.

Original ingredients
watermelon radish
mustard seed
pickled red onion
pink salt

Variation 1
1 green heirloom tomato, sliced
1 tablespoon pickled spring onion (page 31)
¼ teaspoon ground cumin
1 teaspoon chopped fresh cilantro
Black lava salt

Variation 2
3 chive blossoms, roughly chopped
1 teaspoon chopped chives
1 tablespoon chopped fennel fronds
Cyprus flake salt

Mushroom Toast

To make the variations, the original ingredients can be replaced by the alternative options below.

Original ingredients
beech
thyme
sancerre

Variation 1
½ pound (225 g) porcini mushrooms, halved
2 to 3 sprigs rosemary, leaves removed
½ cup (120 ml) Pinot Noir

Variation 2
½ pound (225 g) blue foot mushrooms, trimmed and sliced
2 to 3 fresh shiso leaves
¼ cup (60 ml) mirin

Variation 3
½ pound (225 g) oyster mushrooms, trimmed and separated
½ cup (15 g) fresh parsley leaves
¼ cup (60 ml) sherry

Variation 4
½ pound (225 g) chanterelle mushrooms, trimmed
½ cup (15 g) fresh tarragon leaves
½ cup (120 ml) Chardonnay

Ramp Toast

To make the variations, the original ingredients can be replaced by the alternative options below.

Original ingredients
ramp butter
roasted ramp

Variation 1
½ cup (45 g) blanched and chopped spring onions for the butter
8 ounces (225 g) english runner beans for roasting

Variation 2
¾ cup (45 g) blanched and chopped spring garlic for the butter
4 garlic scapes for roasting

Pan con Tomate

To make the variations, the original ingredients can be replaced by the alternative options below.

Original ingredients
roma tomato
miche

Variation 1
4 indigo rose tomatoes, halved
2 slices sourdough bread

Variation 2
2 large heirloom tomatoes of any color, halved
2 slices rye bread

Eggplant Crostini

To make the variations, the original ingredients can be replaced by the alternative options below. Unlike the tahini, the yogurt and crème fraîche can be used plain, without any additional preparation or ingredients.

Original ingredients
tahini spread
pine nut
pickled red onion

Variation 1
½ cup (120 ml) yogurt, good-quality store-bought or homemade (page 164)
¼ cup (40 g) white sesame seeds
3 to 6 Beet-cured Eggs (page 142), halved

Variation 2
½ cup (120 ml) crème fraîche, good-quality store-bought or homemade (page 164)
¼ cup (30 g) slivered almonds
½ cup (55 g) pickled pearl onions (page 31)

Poached Salmon Toast

To make the variations, the original ingredients can be replaced by the alternative options below.

Original ingredients
salmon
pink salt

Variation 1
2 (8-ounce/225-g) trout fillets
Black lava salt

Variation 2
2 (8-ounce/225-g) sea bass fillets
Smoked salt

Variation 3
2 (8-ounce/225-g) cod fillets
Cyprus flake salt

Cook's Notes – Bowls

Parmesan Brodo

To make the variations, simply replace the spinach with mustard greens or sorrel. If using mustard greens, cook them for 5 to 7 minutes. The sorrel will cook quickly like the spinach (2 to 3 minutes). The radish can be replaced with raw peas or raw asparagus.

Original ingredients
young spinach
radish

Variation 1
3 cups (90 g) mustard greens, chopped
½ cup (75 g) fresh English peas

Variation 2
3 cups (90 g) sorrel
2 white asparagus spears, shaved into ribbons

Everyday Bowl

To make the variations, prepare 1 cup of the alternate grain according to the method in the grain guide on page 25; the original ingredients can be replaced by the alternative options below. The asparagus, beets, and red peppers should not be tossed with maple syrup, but otherwise can be roasted in the same manner as the carrots. For the beets, follow instructions on page 96.

Original ingredients
farro
market radish
roasted purple carrot
piave

Variation 1
1 cup (170 g) quinoa
2 purple spring onions, purple parts only, thinly sliced
1 bunch asparagus, roasted
1 ounce (28 g) shaved Pecorino

Variation 2
1 cup (200 g) millet
1 small bunch lacinato kale, stemmed and roughly chopped
2 medium beets, roasted (page 96)
1 ounce (28 g) shaved Parmesan cheese

Variation 3
1 cup (140 g) bulgur
1 cup (90 g) shaved fennel
1 red pepper, sliced and roasted
1 ounce (30 g) shaved Manchego cheese

White Miso Soup

To make the variations, the original ingredients can be replaced by the alternative options below. Prepare the alternate noodles according to the package directions.

Original ingredients
soba noodle
black trumpet mushroom
bok choy
beet-cured egg

Variation 1
8 ounces (225 g) dried ramen noodles
8 ounces (225 g) shiitake mushrooms, trimmed and sliced
2 handfuls fresh spinach
2 Saffron-cured Eggs (page 142), halved

Variation 2
8 ounces (225 g) dried rice noodles
8 ounces (225 g) cremini mushrooms, trimmed and sliced
4 kale leaves, stemmed
2 Cured Eggs (page 142), halved

Cook's Notes – Plates

Ceviche

To make the variations, the original ingredients can be replaced by the alternative options below.

Original ingredients
halibut
yellowfin tuna
poblano

Variation 1
8 ounces (225 g) grouper
8 ounces (225 g) snapper
¼ head Treviso, shredded

Variation 2
8 ounces (225 g) fluke
8 ounces (225 g) scallops
1 medium avocado, diced

Spring Salad

To make the variations, the original ingredients can be replaced by the alternative options below. Unlike the zucchini, the peas do not need to be shaved into ribbons. The yogurt and crème fraîche should be spread below the peas on your platter.

Original ingredients
zucchini crudo
buffalo mozzarella
lemon balm

Variation 1
2 cups (130 g) purple snow peas
½ cup (30 g) red sorrel
¼ cup (60 ml) plain yogurt, good-quality store-bought or homemade (page 164)
¼ cup (10 g) cilantro flowers

Variation 2
2 cups (175 g) sliced fennel
¼ cup (25 g) shaved Pecorino
¼ cup (10 g) whole fresh basil leaves

Variation 3
2 cups (130 g) sugar snap peas
¼ cup (60 ml) crème fraîche, good-quality store-bought or homemade (page 164)
¼ cup (8 g) whole fresh tarragon leaves

Grilled Octopus

To make the variations, the original ingredients can be replaced by the alternative options below. The caperberries, pickled mustard seeds, or Castelvetrano olives can be braised in the same manner as the black olives (page 140) and added as a garnish to the finished dish. The yogurt, tahini, or eggplant puree can take the place of the crema at the bottom of the platter. Garnish all variations with sea salt and lemon juice.

Original ingredients
burnt citrus crema
braised olive

Variation 1
½ cup (120 ml) plain yogurt, good-quality store-bought or homemade (page 164)
½ cup (85 g) caperberries

Variation 2
½ cup (120 ml) black tahini
½ cup (85 g) Pickled Mustard Seeds (page 32)

Variation 3
½ cup (120 ml) Charred Eggplant Puree (page 138)
½ cup (85 g) Castelvetrano olives

Smoked Black Bread Panzanella

To make the variations, the original ingredients can be replaced by the alternative options below. The carrots and tomatoes can be roasted in the same method as the beets, but will take less time: 20 to 25 minutes total. Do not roast either the mizuna or arugula—simply add it raw to the dish in place of the crispy kale.

Original ingredients
beet
purple kale
radicchio
smoked ricotta

Variation 1
2 bunches carrots, roasted (page 108)
½ head mizuna
1 cup (35 g) watercress
½ cup (120 ml) plain yogurt, good-quality store-bought or homemade (page 164)

Variation 2
2 tomatoes, sliced
2 cups (40 g) arugula
½ cup (20 g) fresh purple basil
8 ounces (225 g) burrata

Deconstructed Niçoise Salad

To make the variations, the original ingredients can be replaced by the alternative options below. The cornichons, capers, and anchovies do not need to be braised.

Original ingredients
market lettuce
halibut
haricot vert
braised olive

Variation 1
2 heads frisée, separated
1 (1-pound/455-g) salmon fillet
4 ounces (115 g) Romano beans
½ cup (70 g) cornichons

Variation 2
3 heads Treviso, separated
1 (1-pound/455-g) tuna fillet
4 ounces (115 g) snow peas
½ cup (90 g) capers

Variation 3
8 to 10 heads mâche, separated
1 (1-pound/455-g) cod fillet
4 ounces (115 g) yellow wax beans
5 marinated anchovies

Cook's Notes – Mains

Whole Fish

To make the variations, simply replace the fish with the following, based on what is fresh at your fish shop, and replace the sumac red onions with fennel or radish as a topping. Because branzini and sea bass are usually smaller than yellowtail snapper, they may take slightly less time to cook.

Original ingredients
yellowtail snapper
sumac red onion

Variation 1
2 whole branzini, about 1 pound (450 g) each, cleaned
1 cup (90 g) pickled fennel (page 31)

Variation 2
2 whole sea bass, about 1 pound (450 g) each, cleaned
1 cup (100 g) shaved radish (shaved on a mandoline)

Sausage

To make the variations, the original ingredients can be replaced by the alternative options below.

Original ingredients
purple cabbage
yogurt
pickled mustard seed

Variation 1
½ head green cabbage, cored and shredded
2 tablespoons Marinated Labneh (page 168)
½ cup (75 g) Pickled Red Onion (page 32)

Variation 2
½ head napa cabbage, cored and shredded
2 tablespoons burnt citrus crema (page 92)
½ cup (75 g) pickled fennel (page 31)

Variation 3
½ head savoy cabbage, cored and shredded
2 tablespoons fromage blanc
½ cup (75 g) pickled radishes (page 31)

Dukkah-Covered Schnitzel

For the variations, assemble the ingredients in the same manner as the original. In the first variation, you do not use dukkah and simply increase the amount of bread crumbs to a total of 1½ cups. In the second variation, you replace both the dukkah and the bread crumbs with the panko.

Original ingredients
earth dukkah + bread crumbs
baby gem lettuce
fennel
pea shoot

Variation 1
1½ cups (135 g) bread crumbs
1 head romaine lettuce, separated
1 cucumber, shaved on a mandoline
2 cups (70 g) watercress

Variation 2
1½ cups (135 g) panko bread crumbs
1 head red leaf lettuce, separated
1 summer squash, shaved on a mandoline
½ cup (30 g) chickweed

Brisket Tacos

To make the variations, the original ingredients can be replaced by the alternative options below.

Original ingredients
napa cabbage
pickled red onion
cotija

Variation 1
2 cups (190 g) shredded purple cabbage
1 cup (75 g) pickled radishes (page 31)
½ cup (50 g) crumbled queso fresco

Variation 2
2 cups (290 g) raw summer corn, cut from the cob
1 cup (75 g) pickled poblanos (page 31)
½ cup (60 g) crumbled queso blanco

Shells

To make the variations, the original ingredients can be replaced by the alternative options below.

Original ingredients
wood ear
oil-cured olive
pecorino

Variation 1
1 pound (455 g) maitake mushrooms, trimmed
1 cup (155 g) Niçoise olives
¼ cup (25 g) finely grated Piave cheese

Variation 2
½ pound (225 g) morel mushrooms, trimmed
1 cup (155 g) Braised Black Olives (page 140)
¼ cup (25 g) finely grated Parmesan cheese

Lasagnette

To make the variations, the original ingredients can be replaced by the alternative options below. These variations, which employ spaghetti and pappardelle, call for a fresh tomato sauce, which can also be used in the original Lasagnette recipe, when tomatoes are in season. To make the sauce, simply substitute peeled fresh tomatoes (Early Girl or Roma work well) for the canned tomatoes. Bring a large pot of water to a boil over high heat. Fill a large bowl with ice water and set it nearby. Cut a large X in the bottom of each tomato and, working in two batches, carefully drop them into the boiling water. Blanch for 30 seconds, then immediately use a slotted spoon to transfer the tomatoes to the ice water to stop the cooking. When cool enough to handle, gently peel the skin from the tomatoes with a paring knife. Use the peeled tomatoes as directed on page 126.

Original ingredients
lasagna noodles
san marzano tomatoes

Variation 1
1 pound (455 g) dried spaghetti
4 pounds (1.8 kg) Early Girl tomatoes

Variation 2
1 pound (455 g) dried pappardelle
4 pounds (1.8 kg) Roma tomatoes

Smoked Ricotta Gnudi

To make the variations, the original ingredients can be replaced by the alternative options below.

Original ingredient
purple basil

Variation 1
Handful of fresh tarragon

Variation 2
Handful of fresh chive blossoms

Variation 3
Handful of fresh flat-leaf parsley

Aged Rib Eye

To make the variations, the original ingredients can be replaced by the alternative options below.

Original ingredients
pink and black peppercorns
lemon balm
watermelon radish

Variation 1
1 teaspoon mixed whole green and black peppercorns, crushed
1 sprig fresh basil
1 black radish, thinly shaved on a mandoline

Variation 2
1 teaspoon whole wild peppercorns, crushed
1 sprig fresh parsley
1 purple radish, thinly shaved on a mandoline

Cook's Notes – Snacks

Cured Eggs

To make the variations, the following can be added to the vinegar mixture and simmered as directed.

Original ingredients
bay leaf

Variation 1 – pink
1 beet, greens removed

Variation 2 – yellow
¼ teaspoon saffron threads

Dukkah

To make the variations, the original ingredients can be replaced by the alternative options below.

Original ingredients
white sesame
coconut flake
pine nut
almond
chamomile

Variation 1 – black
½ cup (60 g) black sesame seeds
2 tablespoons poppy seeds
1 tablespoon pine nuts, lightly toasted and finely chopped
1 tablespoon slivered almonds, finely chopped
5 walnuts, crushed with a mortar and pestle

Variation 2 – green
¼ cup (30 g) pistachios, finely chopped or crushed
⅓ cup (75 g) hemp seeds
⅓ cup (50 g) white sesame seeds
1 tablespoon crushed dried rose petals
½ teaspoon ground cinnamon

Variation 3 – earth
½ cup (60 g) hazelnuts, finely chopped
½ cup (60 g) walnuts, crushed with a mortar and pestle
½ teaspoon coriander seeds, crushed with a mortar and pestle
¼ cup (40 g) white sesame seeds

Desserts

Sahleb

To make the variations, the orange blossom water, agave nectar, or honey can be mixed into the drink before serving, as done with the rose water in the original recipe. All other ingredients can be replaced by the options below, which should be sprinkled on top of the sahleb before serving.

Original ingredients
rose water
coconut
pistachio
ceylon cinnamon

Variation 1
1 teaspoon orange blossom water
2 tablespoons hemp seeds
1 tablespoon white sesame seeds
Sprinkle of freshly grated nutmeg

Variation 2
1 teaspoon agave nectar
2 tablespoons Dukkah (page 146)
1 tablespoon black sesame seeds
Sprinkle of muscovado sugar

Variation 3
1 teaspoon honey
2 tablespoons chopped dried figs
2 tablespoons slivered almonds
Sprinkle of ground ginger

Burnt Apricot

To make the variations, the original ingredients can be replaced by the alternative options below.

Original ingredients
apricot
puffed amaranth

Variation 1
6 nectarines, halved and pitted
¼ cup (40 g) buckwheat, toasted

Variation 2
6 peaches, halved and pitted
¼ cup (4 g) puffed millet

Variation 3
12 figs, halved
¼ cup (35 g) Dukkah (page 146)

Banana Bread

To make the variations, use nuts instead of the chocolate and switch up the garnishes as well, using the alternative options below. Assemble the ingredients in the same manner as the original.

Original ingredients
dark chocolate
crème fraîche
cyprus salt

Variation 1
1 cup (120 g) chopped walnuts
1 to 2 tablespoons plain yogurt, good-quality store-bought or homemade (page 164), per serving
Sprinkle of black salt

Variation 2
1 cup (95 g) sliced almonds
1 to 2 tablespoons Mascarpone, per serving
Sprinkle of pink salt

Dark Chocolate Olive Oil Cake

To make the variations, the original garnish ingredients can be replaced by the following. Instead of making the cardamom cream, garnish each serving with about 1 tablespoon of either plain crème fraîche or Marscapone. Add a sprinkling of flower petals and about 1 tablespoon of nuts on each slice.

Original ingredients
pistachio
rose
cardamom cream

Variation 1
½ cup (60 g) chopped macadamia nuts
1 teaspoon dried or fresh violets
1 cup (240 ml) crème fraîche, good-quality store-bought or homemade (page 164)

Variation 2
½ cup (60 g) chopped hazelnuts
1 teaspoon dried or fresh hibiscus flowers
1 cup (240 ml) Mascarpone

Your Notes

Your Notes

Your Notes

your notes

Your Notes

Basic Ingedients

We feel that a stocked pantry
lends itself to inspired and
delicious meals. From everyday
items to unique finds, here is
a list of some of our favorite
ingredients to keep on hand.

Oils & Vinegars

balsamic vinegar
distilled white vinegar
grapeseed oil
mirin
olive oil (extra-virgin)
red wine vinegar
saba
sherry vinegar
white wine vinegar

Salts

black lava salt
Cyprus flake salt
kosher salt
Peruvian pink salt
sel de Guérande
Sonoma sea salt

Spices

cardamom
cinnamon
coriander
cumin
ginger (fresh, ground)
mahlab
mustard seeds (black, yellow)
nutmeg
peppercorns (black, green, pink)
red pepper flakes
saffron
smoked paprika
sumac
za'atar

Nuts & Seeds

almonds (slivered, raw)
coconut
green almonds
hazelnuts
hemp seeds
macadamia nuts
nigella seeds
pepitas (pumpkin seeds)
pine nuts
pistachios
poppy seeds
sesame seeds (black, white)
sunflower seeds
walnuts

Grains

amaranth
buckwheat
bulgur
farro
long-grain white rice
millet
quinoa
short-grain brown rice

Pantry

chamomile
cocoa nibs
fermented kraut
kombu
maca
miso
orange blossom water
rooibos tea
rose petals (fresh or dried)
rose water
sriracha
tahini

Brined

caperberries
capers
cornichons
olives (black, Castelvetrano,
    oil-cured, Niçoise)
pickles (fruit, vegetable)

Baking

active dry yeast
all-purpose flour
baking powder
baking soda
dark chocolate
rye flour
semolina flour
unsweetened cocoa powder
vanilla beans
vanilla extract

Sweeteners

agave syrup
brown sugar (light, dark)
dark maple syrup
granulated sugar
honeycomb
muscovado sugar
pomegranate molasses
raw honey
superfine sugar

Dairy

almond milk
buffalo butter
butter (salted, unsalted)
buttermilk
cashew milk
coconut milk
crème fraîche
half-and-half
heavy cream
kefir
labneh
sour cream
whole milk
whole yogurt

Cheese

buffalo mozzarella
burrata
cotija
feta
fromage blanc
goat
Manchego
Mascarpone
Parmesan
Pecorino
Piave
queso fresco
ricotta (smoked, fresh)

Fresh Herbs

basil (green, purple)
bay leaf
chervil
chive blossoms
chives
cilantro
cornflower
dill
flowering thyme
hibiscus
kaffir lime
lemon balm
marjoram
mint
nasturtium
oregano
parsley
rosemary
sage
shiso leaves
sorrel
tarragon
thyme
violets

Sources

Pantry

ILĀ
Our own pantry line: a collection of our very favorite spices, salts, and other kitchen essentials, carefully harvested from around the globe.

475 Kent Avenue, Suite 403 | Brooklyn, NY
ila-shop.co
(718) 388-2510

Specialty Breads

Amy's Bread
multiple locations
amysbread.com

Balthazar
80 Spring Street | New York, NY
balthazarbakery.com
(212) 965-1785

Bien Cuit
120 Smith Street | Brooklyn, NY
biencuit.com
(718) 852-0200

High Street on Hudson
637 Hudson Street | New York, NY
highstreetonhudson.com
(917) 388-3944

Pain d'Avignon
multiple locations
paindavignon-nyc.com

Sullivan Street Bakery
multiple locations
sullivanstreetbakery.com

Groceries and Markets

Blue Hill Market at Stone Barns
bluehillmarket.com

Chelsea Market
75 Ninth Avenue | New York, NY
chelseamarket.com
(212) 652-2121

Citarella
multiple locations
citarella.com

Dean & DeLuca
multiple locations
deandeluca.com

Eataly
200 Fifth Avenue | New York, NY
www.eataly.com
(212) 229-2560

Essex Street Market
120 Essex Street | New York, NY
essexstreetmarket.com
(212) 312-3603

Foragers
multiple locations
foragersmarket.com

Greenpoint/McCarren Park Greenmarket
North 12th Street and Union Avenue | Brooklyn, NY
grownyc.org
(212) 788-7476

Union Market
multiple locations
unionmarket.com

Union Square Greenmarket
1 Union Square West | New York, NY
grownyc.org
(212) 788-7476

Whole Foods
multiple locations
wholefoodsmarket.com

Butchers

Fleishers
multiple locations
fleishers.com

Hamlet Meats
hamletmeats.com
(347) 762-3530

Marlow & Daughters
95 Broadway | Brooklyn, NY
marlowanddaughters.com
(718) 388-5700

Meat Hook
397 Graham Avenue | Brooklyn, NY
the-meathook.com
(718) 609-9300

Specialty Cheese and Charcuterie

Bedford Cheese Shop
229 Bedford Avenue | Brooklyn, NY
bedfordcheeseshop.com
(718) 599-7588

Cowgirl Creamery
multiple locations
cowgirlcreamery.com

Murray's Cheese
254 Bleecker Street | New York, NY
murrayscheese.com
(212) 243-3289

Salvatore Ricotta
salvatorebklyn.com

Vermont Creamery
vermontcreamery.com
(800) 884-6287

Other

Mast Brothers
multiple locations
mastbrothers.com

Index

Index

Index

Acknowledgments

This book is a celebration of food, life, and spirit. The hands and love that went into these pages are so important. I have dreamed up this book for many years and feel so humbled and thankful to have it in fruition.

Ken+Sophia, you are my anchors and my allies in everything I do. Sophia, you have successfully tested and tasted almost all of the recipes. You are my greatest audience and my biggest inspiration—in pretty much everything, large and small.

Gracious thanks to Lara Southern (my right-hand lady) and Julia Johnson: Two talented, incredible chicks who helped with heart and soul at each and every turn. Judy Linden, always a phone call away, answering in a heartbeat. Marjolein Delhaas who is so insanely talented she makes you want to do better work.

I'm thankful to the folks at Abrams for allowing this vision to come to life and particularly my editor Laura Dozier for her guidance and support, and always being calm and cool throughout this project.

I feel gratitude to all and to my peers and community who are so very inspiring. It is an incredible moment to be able to articulate your vision and work into a tangible print form. I do hope it lends some inspiration to others as I have been inspired by so many of you.

Thank you all, with a hand to my heart.